N·E·V·A·D·A

Angler's Guide

Fish Tails In The Sagebrush

D1449933

Richard Dickerson

N·E·V·A·D·A
Angler's Guide

Fish Tails In The Sagebrush

Richard Dickerson

Frank
Amato
PORTLAND

Published in 1997 by
Frank Amato Publications, Inc.
PO Box 82112
Portland, Oregon 97282
(503) 653-8108

Softbound
ISBN: 1-57188-100-X
UPC: 0-66066-00294-5

All photographs taken by the author unless otherwise noted.

Book design: Tony Amato

Printed in Canada

10 9 8 7 6 5 4 3 2 1

Contents

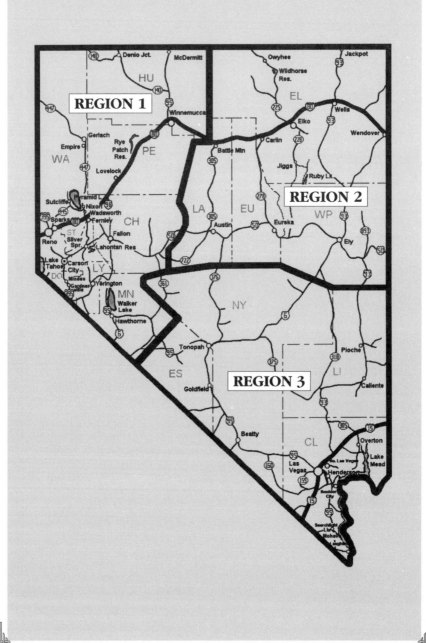

Introduction

To the casual observer, Nevada is a sea of sagebrush. A state famous for its mining, gaming, wedding chapels and quickie divorces. To those who have lived within it borders for a few years, Nevada is a rare outdoor paradise. A paradise that includes unique opportunities for its anglers.

True, Nevada lies in the rain shadow of the towering Sierra Nevada Mountains and only gets nine inches of precipitation a year. It's also true that most of the moisture falls as snow in the state's rugged mountains. Most of the state's fishable water comes directly from snow. After all Nevada in Spanish means snow covered.

Very little precipitation falls on the seventh largest state during the summer. The most arid region of the state is the central and southern third, roughly from Walker Lake south to the Colorado River. On the other hand, the north east is the highest, coolest and wettest part of the state.

Nevada's streams and lakes are mere shadows of the water that once covered this high desert. Many old stream beds swell with run off each spring only to disappear by summer. Some rivers run low except in the spring or during a rare wet year.

Nevada has more mountain ranges than any other state. The state's mountains were formed by shifts in the earth's crust. Called plate tectonics, movement by huge slabs of the earth's crust created the terrain we see today. One edge of the plate tipped up while the other sank. Viewed from over flying aircraft some ridge lines appear as waves frozen in place on a sea of sagebrush.

Nevada's mountain ranges tend to run northeast and southwest and are separated by level-floored valleys. Stand in any of the long Nevada valleys and you'll realize that erosion has leveled their floors. Deep cuts in the flanks of the mountains are the scars left by that erosion. It is a process than has taken several thousand years. Over 2,760 miles of streams still flow from these mountains.

Nevada's state flower and most common plant is the sagebrush. It grows everywhere except in the white, alkali flats and on the alpine peaks. Sagebrush covers nearly 50 percent of the state. Most of the mountains are covered with juniper and pinon woodlands. In the high country, aspen, lodgepole pine, sugar pine and mountain mahogany grow. Coyotes, jackrabbits and mule deer are the most common mammals travelers see. Spend time in Nevada and you'll see some of the state's 50 reptile species.

Despite the state's desert appearance, Nevada was once home to the largest cutthroat trout in the world. About 70,000 years ago, Lake Lahontan covered more than 8,000 square miles of northern Nevada. This is when cutthroat trout most likely entered the state from the Snake River system.

By the time the first Europeans entered the state, native cultures had evolved around the cutthroat fishery. When John C. Freemont found Pyramid Lake in 1844, he described the fish as "salmon-trout" and compared their size to Columbia River salmon—two to four feet long. The official record Lahontan cutthroat weighed in at 41 pounds. It is shadowed by unconfirmed catches of fish estimated in the 60-pound range.

That original race of Pyramid Lake cutthroat became extinct during the 1940s. Demands for water deprived the cutthroat of their upstream spawning grounds.

Such is the tale of many of Nevada's fisheries. The growth brought on first by mining booms, gold, silver and copper to name a few and later with gambling, put fish and their habitat low on the list of priorities. During the last few decades, however, that has begun to change in Nevada as with the rest of America. People have placed a higher value on clean water, a pristine environment and wildlife.

Anglers casting a line in Nevada's waters today enjoy a variety of angling opportunities. Cold water fisheries hold rainbow trout, brown trout, cutthroat trout, bull trout, kokanee and mackinaw. Warmer water fisheries have smallmouth bass, largemouth bass, white bass, striped bass, walleye, perch and catfish. In between are hybrids like bow-cuts, tiger trout and wipers.

In 1987, the Nevada Division of Wildlife produced a brochure called "Fishable Waters of Nevada." It lists 509 fishable streams and 125 fishable lakes and reservoirs. This book will not cover all those waters. Instead the criteria for getting into this book is: good public access (driving or walking) and the fishing can take the pressure without suffering.

What the reader will find in these pages is a description of the stream, lake or reservoir, directions on how to get there, and what to expect in the way of fishing and services. A separate chapter covers getting around Nevada. Contacts and phone numbers are provided to help plan your next Nevada fishing trip. The last chapter is a look inside this Nevada angler's fly box. Favorite patterns and how to tie them is not the only subject. Included is a description of rigging tackle and fishing tactics.

Most angling secrets, however, are sweeter when discovered by fishermen seeking new waters. Nevada holds many unique angling opportunities for its fishermen. Each outing is a chance to discover something new and exciting. Let this book be your guide on that road of discovery. But do not stop here. Go out and explore the sagebrush sea and discover its fishing for yourself.

From the sagebrush sea, 1996

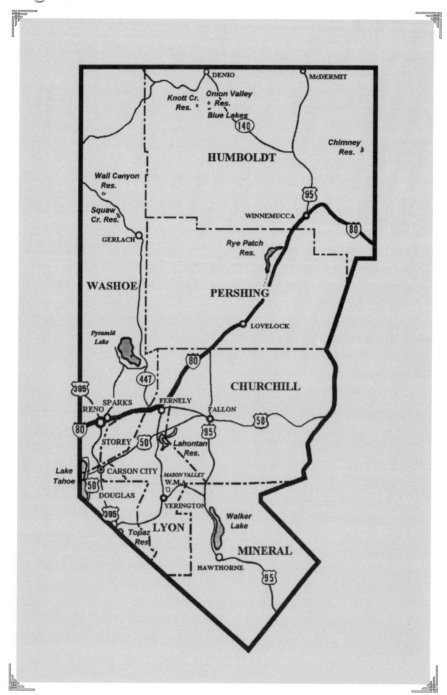

Region 1

All of the northwest third of Nevada falls within the boundaries on Region 1. Nevada's Division of Wildlife biologists responsible for these waters travel through some of the state's biggest deserts. They also manage the state's heaviest fished urban waters. Three major rivers start in California.

Region 1 includes Reno and Sparks. As Nevada's second largest metropolitan area, these cities occupy the Truckee Meadows and are divided by the Truckee River. Also in Region 1 is the state capitol Carson City. Named for the famous scout and frontiersman Kit Carson, the Carson River is another urban stream. The third major stream in this region is the Walker River. This river bares the name of another explorer and mountain man, Joe Walker. The East and West Walker Rivers join near the agricultural and mining community of Yerington.

Interstate 80 is the major east-west route in Region 1. U.S. Highway 50, however, leads to most of the better fisheries in Lyon and Churchill counties. The north-south routes of importance to anglers are U.S. Highway 447 north from I-80 at Wadsworth, Alternate Highway 95 south from Fernley and Highway 95.

Excellent accommodations, hotels and restaurants abound in Reno and Sparks. Carson City, Minden and Gardnerville also offer excellent services for traveling anglers. Along I-80 there are many gas-food-bed stops. The rural areas of northern Washoe, Humboldt and southern Lyon Counties have limited services.

CHAPTER 1: Washoe County

Reno and Sparks, Nevada's second largest population center, is situated in southern Washoe County. The northern portion of this political entity reaches to the Oregon border and includes broad alkali basins.

For the angler, Washoe holds some of the state's better fishing. The Truckee River is an impressive stream that flows through the Biggest Little City In The World—Reno. Pyramid Lake is the ancestral home of world record cutthroat trout. Two man-made reservoirs in the arid northern portion of the county offer good to excellent trout fishing. Topping this off is a handful of high Sierra trout streams for anglers who like to explore.

Accommodations in the Reno-Sparks area fit every budget category. The farther the angler travels from this center of commerce and tourism, the more rustic the accommodations and the more primitive the camping.

Truckee River

The Truckee River was the breeding ground of giant Lahontan cutthroat trout. Every fall, about Thanksgiving Day, the big cutts, driven by the need to spawn, entered the river from Pyramid Lake. In some cases, the trout would swim most of the 115 miles to Lake Tahoe. Early Truckee Meadows residents claimed "you could walk across the river on the backs of fish."

Now, over 50 years later, the river still can support big trout. As recently as the early 1980s brown trout over 10 pounds were caught in downtown Reno. During the recent prolonged drought, however, the river and its fish have suffered. Back to back wet years are needed to restore Nevada's best urban fishery.

The Truckee starts high in the Sierra as a tributary from Lake Tahoe. On the river's journey to its termination at Pyramid Lake, it drops 2,500 feet in elevation. Two thirds of the drop is in the Truckee Canyon between Lake Tahoe and Reno. At Derby Dam, about 17 miles east of Sparks, most of the river is diverted to Lahontan Reservoir and the Carson River. At Wadsworth, the river turns north and enters the Pyramid Lake Indian Reservation.

From the California border downstream three miles is the trophy section of the river. Here tackle restrictions permit trout to grow big and smart. General

Facing Page: Snow replenishes the Truckee River.
Cold nights line the shallow banks with ice.

limits and tackle restrictions apply on the remainder of the Truckee until it enters the Pyramid Lake Indian Reservation.

The Truckee is easily accessible for the majority of its 75-mile Nevada journey. Private property on the banks of the river does restrict access in some areas however. Anglers who insist on crossing railroad tracks or climbing fences around diversion dams take unnecessary risks. A little walking or wading will cover all the river's best holds.

Around Verdi, anglers gain access at Crystal Peak Park, Dog Valley Road bridge and both of the Third Street bridges. If unsure about where to go, ask at Reno area sporting goods stores.

Nearer Reno is Mayberry Park. Here is a strip of good access to great fishing. Regular fish plantings, tall cottonwood trees and picnic benches make the park a good place for a family outing. Within Reno is Idlewild Park. Another spot for a family fishing experience. Between Reno and Sparks are three more access points called Fisherman's Park. Fishermen can find more places to wet a line without infringing on private property.

Angler survey data from 1993 revealed that Truckee River fishermen averaged 2.38 fish per day. While many of the 248,901 fish caught in 1993 were likely planted fish, the 26- and 24-inch brown trout landed the next

Drought affects trout, isects and the way anglers approach the water.

Water diversions continue though the Truckee River runs low during a continuing drought.

year were not. There is some natural spawning in the Truckee when water flows permit.

During 1994, Nevada stocked the Truckee River below the trophy section with 84,586 catchable rainbow trout, 17,696 catchable brown trout and 4,020 catchable cutthroat trout. In addition, 15,026 juvenile brown trout and 29,300 juvenile cutthroat were placed in the river.

Mountain whitefish are an overlooked Truckee River sport fish. Bonier than their trout cousins, whitefish are more active during winter months when trout become dormant. Fly fishing for whitefish with thin tippets and light tackle is challenging.

Fly fishing on the Truckee River rivals many of the popular waters in neighboring states. The river is home to most of the aquatic insects fly fishermen like to imitate. Golden stoneflies are the biggest. Little yellow stones produce exciting late evening hatches from June through August and into September.

Several species of caddisfly call the river home too. The Truckee River Special was designed to imitate the spotted sedge. Mayflies are not as abundant now as 20 years ago because of pollution and low water conditions. Still good hatches come off frequently.

Two species of suckers and the Paiute sculpin also live in the Truckee. Streamer fishermen imitating these big bite foods can entice some of the river's biggest trout to strike.

Bouncing salmon eggs and worms always work in the Truckee. The trick as with any river is to get down to the fish. Using minnows is legal, but check the regulations and deal only with a licensed bait shop to avoid a costly fine.

Panther Martin and Mepps lures work year-round in the Truckee. Big trout hunters looking for fall-spawning brown trout use big Rebels and Rapalas.

Pyramid Lake

Pyramid Lake is big fish and big water. This lake is home to the largest cut-throat trout in the world, but it is a fall-winter-spring fishery. The season opens in October and closes in May.

Five-pound trout are common and 10-pound fish are landed every season at Pyramid. In April 1994, a 21-pound 4-ounce cutthroat was taken by a wading fly fishermen. The lake's official record is 44 pounds but historians argue that 60-pound-plus fish once inhabited the lake.

Before the original race of cutthroat became extinct in 1940, thousands of pounds of fish were shipped to Salt Lake City and San Francisco every year. Cutthroat were re-established in the 1960s, but today the fish are sustained by hatcheries.

About 8,000 years ago ancient Lake Lahontan became the desert we know today as Northern Nevada. Pyramid is a remnant of that lake. Today, Pyramid Lake has 70 miles of shoreline. The lake lies totally inside the Pyramid Lake Reservation. The tribe sells permits for fishing, camping and boating. Two improved boat ramps on the west shore open the lake to fishermen. One landing is at the Sutcliffe Marina and the

John Van Emmerik admires a 6-pound Pyramid Lake cutthroat trout.

other is farther north at Pelican Point. Private campgrounds are available in Sutcliffe on the lake's western shore. Tribal permits allow camping in other areas around the lake. All types of restaurants and hotels are available in Reno and Sparks.

Pyramid Lake is located 30 miles north of Sparks via Highway 445, or from Interstate 80 and Wadsworth, take Highways 447 and 446. Improved dirt roads flank the northern end of the lake and most of the eastern shore. Roads do not completely circle the lake, however. Wander off the hard surfaced roads and you are likely to get stuck in the fine sand.

There is more than one way to approach shore fishing at Pyramid Lake, 30 miles north of Reno, Nevada.

At times trollers using large spoons, Flat Fish or other lures do better than shore anglers. During fall, trolling along deep water drop-offs is the popular technique. A favorite area is the northeastern corner of the lake known as Hell's Kitchen. This area has shear cliffs of white tufa rock and during bad weather earns its name. Anglers should cross the lake only in large boats.

During the spawning season, late march to season closing, shore fishermen catch more trout. The big trout cruise in and out of the shallows in unpredictable patterns. The secret is to have your fly or lure in the water when the fish are there. Some shore anglers move every hour or so if they don't get a strike. Lure-casting shore fishermen use number 2 spoons in fluorescent green or red. Fly fishermen do the same thing with dark and bright Woolly Worms on a two-fly cast. Fly casters, however, put their offering on the sandy bottom. A fast-sinking shooting head rig is standard fly fishing gear at Pyramid.

The main food source for the trout is the lake's tui chub. This minnow provides the protein necessary to support the big trout.

Pyramid is the fishery of choice during winter. Therefore most Reno and Sparks area tackle dealers keep close tabs on the lake and its fish.

Squaw Valley Reservoir

North of Pyramid Lake lies a series of playa lakes known as the Black Rock and Smoke Creek Deserts. Shallow lakes during a wet spring and fine-powdered alkali valleys by late summer, these valleys spread northeast and west from Highway 447 between Empire and Gerlach. There are two reasons a fisherman would drive across this country. One is to find someplace to fish and the other is to see the desert. This first reason is primary.

North of Reno 124 miles and 17 miles north of Gerlach is Squaw Valley Reservoir. Small at 47 1/2 surface acres and 45 feet deep, Squaw holds promise for anglers. The reservoir holds cold-water fish such as rainbow trout—reported catches to 23 inches—cutthroat and browns. It also has largemouth bass—reports up to 5 pounds with 4 pounds verified—green sunfish and brown bullhead catfish. During 1993, a total of 1,729 anglers spent 6,073 days at Squaw Valley and caught 22,258 fish.

Two intermittent streams and several springs enter the reservoir from the north end. Squaw Creek originates from a spring in a meadow north of the reservoir. Other than the large meadow, the surrounding vegetation is sagebrush which means bring your own shade if you want any.

Aquatic vegetation in the shallow warm north end attracts the bass and sunfish. The deeper water near the dam attracts the trout. During summer thick rafts of algae form on the lake's surface.

Fly fishermen should bring patterns that imitate damselflies, dragonflies, midges, snails and water boatmen. Most popular lures and bait rigs work at Squaw Valley.

This reservoir is on private land, but is open to the public and stocked by the Nevada Division of Wildlife. The landowner, however, has expressed an interest in the past in charging a fee for camping on the land next to the lake. At last report camping in unimproved sites was still available. However, bring your water and be prepared to rough it (no services). Some accommodations, restaurants and stores, are available in Gerlach.

Wall Canyon Reservoir

Another reason to drive north of Pyramid Lake on Nevada Highway 447 is Wall Canyon Reservoir. The Wall is located 58 miles north of Gerlach and eight miles east of Highway 447.

The water here is muddy most of the year and the stream is not very productive, but the reservoir holds rainbow, brown, cutthroat trout and smallmouth bass. Aquatic plants also are sparse due to limited light penetration into the reservoir. As you would expect, crayfish are abundant here. Insect life includes midges, damselflies, scuds, mayflies, water boatmen and even caddisflies.

Wall Canyon has 133 surface acres and is 55 feet deep when full. The lake does drop about 10 feet during irrigation season. Boats with outboard motors are allowed, but there are speed limits and they are enforced.

The terrain surrounding Wall Canyon Reservoir is similar to Squaw Valley Reservoir. Camping is permitted, but it is unimproved and during a wet spring it can be very muddy. You won't find an improved boat ramp, so keep the water-craft small.

Yes, Wall Canyon Reservoir is remote, but it is that very trait that makes it a good fishery. If you take time to visit Wall Canyon you could find some good trout fishing. During fall, chukar hunters visit the reservoir as a change of pace.

Washoe County's Small Streams

Stand anywhere in Reno or Sparks and you will see mountains. South of the Truckee River and west of the Truckee Meadows, the mountains are called the Carson Range. Mount Rose and Slide Mountain are the dominant peaks in a mountain range that runs south to Lake Tahoe.

In the Carson Range, within driving distance of Reno, are six small trout streams worthy of an angler's attention. None is a major fishery, but each is an opportunity to explore new waters within easy reach of a major city. There are others the truly adventurous will find, but try these first. Reports about these streams will normally be spotty in Reno area sporting goods stores. These aren't the big draw waters. However, if the Truckee River is fishing well, these streams will to.

Hunter Creek

Located on the north end of the Carson Range, Hunter Creek has just over six miles of fishable water. At the 8,400 elevation brook trout dominate. Closer to the Truckee River and west of Reno near Mayberry Park, just before the creek is diverted, rainbow become the prominent fish. The stream, according to stream survey reports, averages 9 1/2 feet wide and just under six inches deep. The average gradient from beginning to end is eight percent. According to the same survey, Hunter has 633 brook trout per mile and 264 rainbow trout per mile.

Willow, black cottonwood, alder and lodgepole pine add to the scenery high up the canyon. Near the river, sagebrush, bitterbrush and mountain mahogany dominate the landscape.

Insects identified in University of Nevada studies include:		
Caddisflies:	Green Rock Worm	
	Spotted Sedge	
	Cinnamon Sedge	
Stoneflies:	Golden Stone	
	Little Green Stone	
Mayflies:	Pale Morning Dun	
	Pale Evening Dun	
	Blue-wing Olive	
	Gray Drake	
Other:	Water Beetles	

Two-wheel-drive access is limited near the Truckee River due to private property. Even four-wheel-drive is limited near the creek's headwaters and Hunter Lake (a big beaver pond). Hikers, however, can walk into the lower parts of Hunter Canyon and work their way up stream.

This land is part of the Toiyabe National Forest so camping is permitted, but be extremely careful with fires. Avoid fires and limit camping to areas well back from the water. Hunter Creek is great for a day of hiking and fishing.

Thomas Creek

Follow the foothills of the Carson Range as they turn south and you'll find Thomas Creek. Highway 431, Mount Rose Highway to the locals, roughly parallels the creek. Turn north at Timberline Drive. Only 7.7 miles of the stream is fishable because the stream flows through private land. The public sections are in the Toiyabe Forest. Most of the fishable water is accessible by two-wheel-drive, but a four-wheel-drive is advisable for the upper reaches.

During the last stream survey in 1978, Thomas Creek had 580 brook trout per mile and 539 rainbow trout per mile. Again, brookies like the higher altitudes. Rainbow trout are stocked annually, usually in May and June.

There are old signs of beaver activity near the creek, but no dams. Streamside vegetation includes willows, aspens and mixed Jeffrey pine. Sagebrush and bitterbrush start appearing near the mouth of the canyon. Most of the stream is narrow, averaging seven feet wide and bushy. Dapping is the best tactic whether bait or fly fishing. The stream's average depth of 5.2 inches means Thomas Creek lacks quality trout pools. That's the only drawback to this stream.

The aquatic insects living in Thomas Creek are similar to Hunter Creek.

Camping is permitted along Thomas Creek. Occasionally, an inconsiderate camper leaves his trash behind, but that's not a common occurrence. Most level ground is fairly close to the water. The stream averages an 8.4 percent gradient.

Whites Creek

Whites Creek is almost a duplicate of Thomas Creek. Whites runs through the next canyon south of Thomas. In fact you drive across it getting to Thomas Creek. The problem is one gate leads to someone's home and the other leads to National Forest land.

You cannot drive right up to the water, but you can get close with a four-wheel-drive. The road goes almost as far up the canyon as Thomas Creek's road, however, and walking is the best way in.

Camping, insects and fishing tactics all parallel Thomas Creek. The fish, however, are fewer than in Thomas. During the 1978 stream survey, Whites Creek had only 79 fish per mile. Whites and Thomas creeks both receive annual trout plantings.

Galena Creek

High in the Carson Range, 9,280 feet, Galena Creek begins as a trickle. The little stream travels 16.3 miles before losing its identity in other waters. Just over eight miles of Galena is fishable. The creek's average width is 10 1/2 feet and averages six inches deep.

Steeper than its neighbors Whites and Thomas creeks, Galena is also the site of rural development. Access is available on the uphill side of Highway 431, but limited among the homes on the downhill side. Camping is not available on Galena Creek as the county park closes at 7 pm.

The Division of Wildlife's 1978 stream survey recorded 182 brook trout per mile. The fish averaged 2 to 12 inches in length. Galena is also planted with rainbow trout in May and June.

Ophir Creek

Ophir begins as a diversion of Third Creek near Highway 431 on the west side of the Mount Rose summit. This creek flows through Tahoe Meadows before dropping into upper and lower Prices Lakes. Eventually, the stream crosses Highway 395 on its way to Washoe Lake.

There are 5.8 fishable miles of stream here, but the gradient averages 13 percent. The average width of 6.2 feet and average depth of six inches should tell you to expect few pools in the steep canyon below Prices Lakes.

The 1978 stream survey, however, recorded 369 brook trout per mile and

106 rainbow trout per mile. In the Tahoe Meadows portion of the stream, most fish were small, showing this as a nursery for brook trout.

Road access is limited to the Mount Rose Highway and Highway 395. Hiking is the best way to get to this stream. Old fire rings indicate the area is open to camping, but summer brings extreme fire hazards to the Carson Range. Anglers should avoid campfires.

Fly fishermen should carry patterns matching the insects listed under Thomas Creek. Lure fishermen should carry ultralight tackle. Bait fishing with worms and salmon eggs always produces.

Prices Lakes didn't receive separate listing in this book because of a huge landslide that fell into the lake. The lake was reconstructed (a new dam) and is currently about half its former size. Nevada's Division of Wildlife annually stocks the lake with four-inch Tahoe strain rainbow trout.

Franktown Creek

This brook trout stream originates from Hobart Reservoir. Access is available via Hobart—if you don't spend all your time fishing the reservoir.

Franktown has almost seven miles of fishable water from Hobart through Little Valley and down to the 5,200-foot elevation. This stream averages 8 1/2 feet wide and about five inches deep. Camping is limited, as is the stream's access.

There are, however, 943 brook trout per mile on average. These aren't big fish by some standards, but just right for this picturesque stream. Use the same tactics as the other streams listed here, but add grasshoppers in the fall.

CHAPTER 2: Humboldt County

Though named for the river that guided California-bound emigrants across three quarters of Nevada, Humboldt County covers much of ancient Lake Lahontan's dry lake beds. The Humboldt River is still the major east-west route across the sagebrush sea.

Winnemucca is a mandatory stop on long distance drives across Nevada. Gas, food and accommodations draw most travelers from the concrete Interstate 80. Nevada anglers, however, have another reason to turn off at Winnemucca. U.S. Highway 95 north of Winnemucca leads to some of the Silver State's best fishing. Read on, then pack your rod.

Big Springs Reservoir

Nevada is a boom or bust state. Whether mining, gaming or fishing, conditions fulfill your wildest fantasies or they break your heart.

Big Springs Reservoir is a boom or bust reservoir. Located 10 miles from the Oregon border on Nevada Highway 140, Big Springs was originally built for irrigation. Today it is used for wildlife and recreation. The wildlife lives in the Charles Sheldon Antelope Range. The recreation is fishing.

During the 1980s, before the seven-year drought, Big Springs produced 18- to 20-inch trout. Big Springs was a total loss during the winter of 1988-1989. During 1992, the main spring and bank spring were totally dry.

An extremely wet winter in 1994-1995 put water back into the 116 surface acre reservoir. But, because the water averages only nine feet deep, fishing has been slow to improve. A partially full reservoir means turbid water. Since Big Springs is so shallow, the wind can turn the water chocolate colored. Wind is common along the rolling hills and plateaus of the Sheldon Range. Even when the wind lets the silt return to the bottom, the water isn't exactly clear.

Trout do grow, however, as much as half an inch per month. By the fall of 1995, fish stocked in the spring could reach the 16-inch range. If the winters continue to leave near average precipitation, big trout will return to Big Springs.

The tule-lined lake has an abundance of rooted aquatic vegetation. If the sun penetrates the turbid waters, there is lots of vegetation. Because the entire lake acts like one big littoral zone, insects abound. Damselflies, mayflies

(*Callibaetis*), leeches and snails provide most of the fishes forage. Even the high desert wind brings in terrestrial insects.

Camping at Big Springs Reservoir is one step above primitive. There are two fiberglass toilet facilities along the southern shore. Only waist-high sagebrush is available for shade, so bring a hat, an umbrella or awning.

Fishing from a float tube is a good Big Springs tactic, but only when the reservoir is nearly full. Boats without motors are an alternative.

Blue Lakes

A few thousand years ago, after the Pine Forest Mountain Range was formed, glaciers carved out Blue Lakes. The area still gets about 30 inches of precipitation annually, but the glaciers are gone. The winters, however, are tough as these lakes are more than 8,000 feet above sea level.

Blue Lakes attracts anglers and hikers because of its wilderness qualities. The typography includes steep alpine slopes. Substantial stands of mahogany approach the water and willows grow close to the shoreline. Low-growing sagebrush grows in the higher elevation and big sagebrush inhabits lower locations.

A self-sustaining population of brook trout inhabits the lakes, along with cutthroat, bowcut (rainbow-cutthroat hybrid) and tiger trout (brook-brown hybrid). Anglers should be aware that winter kills can pose a problem at Blue Lakes, especially during long, severe winters.

Mayflies (*Callibaetis*) and midges provide most of the trouts' forage. The lakes do have a few dragon- and damselflies, but the lack of emergent vegetation appears to impact their number. Also, scuds inhabit the lakes and the fish will feed on them.

The drive from Winnemucca via U.S. 95 and Highway 140 to Denio Junction is about 100 miles. There, Nevada 140 turns west and roughly parallels the Oregon border for 44 miles. Thirteen miles past Denio Junction look for a green sign with white lettering announcing Knott Creek. Turn south on an improved dirt road for another 15 miles.

As you approach a large alkali lake on the right, look for a brown and white Bureau of Land Management sign on the left. The sign marks the left turn to Onion Valley Reservoir, eight miles and Knott Creek Reservoir, nine miles. Turn left onto this one lane graded road and prepare to climb into the Pine Forest Range. In foul weather, spring and fall, four-wheel-drive vehicles have been known to use tire chains on all four. The top inch or two of soil, when it gets wet, fills the tire treads and makes for a wild drive. High ground clearance, two-wheel-drive vehicles can make the drive into Onion Valley Reservoir, but passenger cars should not try. From there a 20-minute hike over a good trail takes you to Blue Lakes.

Onion Valley Reservoir

An earthen dam reservoir built in 1955 created Onion Valley Reservoir on public land. The water comes from Blue Lakes and springs and is stored for irrigation.

Onion Valley is characteristic of many high-desert reservoirs. Severe winters and summer algae blooms contribute to the lake's rises and falls. Still the rainbow trout grow an average of 0.40 inches per month. Many fish achieve a near football shape. The state record trout for this water is a 17 1/2-inch brook trout taken in 1981. Recent fishing seasons, normally the second Saturday in June through November 15, have seen a variety in the size of trout. This means the lake is healthy and this year's small trout grow to be next season's big fish.

At 101 surface acres, Onion Valley is 42 feet deep near the dam. The elevation is 7,065 feet and is 800 vertical feet below Blue Lakes. Only 21 percent of the lake is over 30 feet deep which means Onion Valley has a large littoral zone. Insect life includes back swimmers, scuds, mayflies, including *Caenis* and damselflies. Boating is allowed, but there is a five nautical mile-per-hour speed limit.

Drive north of Winnemucca approximately 130 miles via Highways 93 and 140 to reach Onion Valley Reservoir. Turnoff Highway 140, 13 miles east of Denio Junction. Go south at the Knott Creek sign and follow the two lane improved dirt road for 15 miles. A brown and white Bureau of Land Management sign on the left marks the Onion Valley turn. Four-wheel-drive and tire chains are recommended when the road is wet or thunderstorms threaten.

Camping is permitted near the water, but there are few amenities here. Primitive conditions prevail. Bring your food, water and shade. Also plan to carry out what you bring in.

Knott Creek Reservoir

Southwest of Blue Lakes and Onion Valley Reservoir sits another excellent trout fishery. An extremely popular area water, Knott Creek, thanks to a new Bureau of Land Management road, is more accessible to Nevada anglers. Fishermen must drive around and through some steep and rocky terrain, however. This is a four-wheel-drive road even in dry weather. Follow the directions listed in Blue Lakes and Onion Valley Reservoir. The Knott Creek Reservoir turn is clearly marked.

In spring, a soggy meadow limits access. Expect a rutted road later in the year as anxious fishermen want to get to Knott Creek as soon as possible. A special catch-and-release-only season runs from the second Saturday in May through the second Friday in June. The normal season opens the following Saturday, but check the regulations for changes.

Knot Creek Reservoir has a good population of big trout as this 20-inch-plus fish verifies.

At Knott Creek, a phenomenal growth rate of 0.68 inches per month means fat trout. Rainbow are the dominant game fish and 3,361 were stocked in 1993. The harvest of fish over 18 inches was 606 fish in 1992 and 1,659 fish in 1993. Anglers land 20-inch-plus fish, but biologists are concerned the size of the trout means few young fish live in the lake.

A rich aquatic environment is responsible for the phenomenal growth of the trout. Mayflies (*Callibaetis*), midges, damsels, dragons, scuds and snails all live in the lake. Also, the fish key in on a blood midge hatch in spring. By mid-July the adult damsels are prolific in blue, green and a few gray ones too. There is also a large population of leeches in the lake.

Fishermen can use a boat and a motor, but a five nautical mile-per-hour speed limit is enforced. Camping is allowed, but primitive. The eastern shore has the better camping, but if the lake is full access is difficult at best. Bring your water and plan on hauling out your trash.

Knott Creek is also a good fall trout lake. Catch rates of 2.85 fish per hour were documented in fall of 1993.

Facing Page:
The first view of Knott Creek Reservoir from the four-wheel-drive road leading to the lake.

Chimney Dam Reservoir

When Chimney Dam was built, Nevada hoped to develop a new cutthroat trout fishery. Unfortunately, turbid water filled the reservoir. Suspended clays and silt from upstream riparian habitat erosion limits the lake's productivity. Light cannot penetrate deep enough to support plant and insect life. As a result a warm-water fishery was established.

Chimney Dam Reservoir is big. Its surface size is 4,600 acre feet, but it is only 47 feet deep. Both the North and South Forks of the Little Humboldt River back up behind the dam.

White crappie are the dominant game fish through their shear numbers. In 1995, the crappie averaged 7 1/4 inches with the largest reaching 9 1/2 inches. Not bad for crappies in northern Nevada. During the 1980s, before the most recent and prolonged Nevada drought, crappie fishing at Chimney Dam Reservoir was exceptional. Fluctuating water levels during the dry period has interrupted spawning cycles.

Walleye are the most sought after game fish in the reservoir today. These 18- to 19-inch predators feed on suckers, speckled dace and other minnows during the spring and summer months. They also eat crappie. In the fall walleye feed heavily on crayfish that populate the lake. Some of the most successful angling for walleye is with crayfish. People catch the soft-shell crayfish in the fall, tail them and freeze them for use next spring. A good crayfish lure or fly pattern can produce too.

Surprisingly, the largemouth bass fishery has never taken off at Chimney Dam. Fisheries workers stocked two separate species of largemouth, Alabama spotted bass and northern largemouth, but they have had limited success. Low reservoir productivity due to turbid water is one reason. Another is the early irrigation season reservoir drawdowns while bass are preparing to spawn or are actually on the nest.

Under normal Chimney Dam conditions, the fishing is best during spring through June. Pre-spawn walleye males and pre-spawn crappie move into the shoals of the two inlets. The last hurrah is the catfish spawn normally along the beaches between the Little Humboldt's Forks.

An excellent boat ramp is available at Chimney Dam. It allows larger boats to launch during low-water conditions. A boat is necessary to reach the North Fork as the area is closed to foot traffic because of private property.

Anglers reach Chimney Dam Reservoir by taking U.S. 95 north from Winnemucca and turning east on Nevada 290 to Paradise Valley. Here the road turns to graded gravel and the signs become a little skimpy. The reservoir is roughly 22 miles southwest of Paradise Valley.

The Santa Rosa Mountains

Like an island in a rolling sea of sagebrush, the Santa Rosa Range attracts attention. Commuters traveling between Winnemucca, Nevada and Boise, Idaho, however, don't realize what is hiding a few miles from U.S. Highway 95. Santa Rosa Peak, for example, stands 9,701 feet tall. This peak along with Buckskin Mountain and a few others, collects a lot of winter's snow. From their flanks spring no less than six fishable streams. One is possibly the best brown trout river in Nevada. The three described here are the biggest and most accessible.

Except for the Martin Creek Campground, all Santa Rosa camping is primitive. Bring everything and carry out the trash.

Martin Creek

Two small headwater tributaries on the eastern side of Buckskin Mountain form upper Martin Creek. From its 8,000-foot beginning, Martin Creek gains volume from Siard, Cabin, Long Valley, Dutch John, Deep and Round Corral creeks. The creek enters a steep, rocky gorge near Coon Flat before turning west toward Paradise Valley. The gorge is extremely rugged and only the most prepared angler should attempt the hike in. Most of the access is upstream of the gorge.

The entire stream is over 48 miles long. The U.S. Forest Service controls just over 15 miles of stream and the Bureau of Land Management another five miles. Much of the remaining privately-held stream is accessible however. Twenty-five miles of Martin Creek is fishable.

Take U.S. 95 from downtown Winnemucca north. Nevada Highway 290 intersects U.S. 95 some 22 miles north of the city. When you arrive in Paradise Valley, a small ranching and farming community, you must decide where to fish. The lower stream is east of Paradise via the improved dirt Chimney Dam Road. After the road leaves the valley the Martin Creek road turns east. The road is unmarked except for a yellow and black sign that warns you a four-wheel-drive is needed 24 miles farther on. Don't worry, a good ground clearance, two-wheel-drive will take you to Hardscrabble. This turn too is unmarked. Look for the second road beyond the underground gas line. This turn takes you to the creek, but it is on private property. Access closer to Paradise Valley is available near Old Mill Ranch. Be sure to respect the landowner's rights or you may not get to come back.

The Hinkey Summit Road from Paradise Valley reaches upper Martin Creek. This too is a two-wheel-drive dirt road, but a steep climb to the 7,867-foot pass. There is a Humboldt National Forest Ranger Station and Campground just

Mark Mahaffey fishes a pool on Martin Creek near the site of Hardscrabble.

beyond the summit. Private cabins follow Martin Creek down from the summit for about seven miles, but better access is available farther on.

Martin Creek has brown, rainbow and hybrid bowcutt trout. Speckled dace, redside shiners and suckers provide forage. This means streamer flies and small spinners produce trout.

Important insects include cased caddis, mayflies, damselflies and grasshoppers. Fly fishermen should not pass this stream. Occasional stands of willow require a shorter than normal leader. Muddlers consistently pull trout from under cut banks and root tangles. Humpy dry flies drifted through the same areas early or late in the day work too.

North Fork Little Humboldt River

Remote streams make good fishing. The North Fork of the Little Humboldt River is a remote stream. There is very little access except at Chimney Dam Reservoir, Greely Crossing, Forks Ranch and Holloway Meadows. Most of the river runs through a deep gorge with spectacular 200- to 300-foot cliffs on both sides.

From Paradise Valley, Nevada Highway 290, take the Chimney Dam improved dirt road. This road takes you to the reservoir and Forks Ranch. This is the lower end of the North Fork gorge.

The shortest route to the upper end of the gorge is over Hinkey Summit from Paradise Valley. Drive past Martin, Cabin and Siard creeks. Bear north and east to reach Holloway Meadows and the upper end of the North Fork. From here the road parallels the river for three miles and crosses the stream above Goosey Lake Flat. Continue over Mahogany Summit then turn south to Greely Crossing.

All 48 miles of the North Fork is considered fishable. Some portions of stream have intermittent flows, especially during long droughts. Still the river has brook, cutthroat and brown trout. Browns dominate. The cutthroat, though native, have interbred with the rainbows.

Beaver dams provide good pools in the upper reaches of the river. Willows provide food for the beaver and frustrate fishermen. Still, if you want to avoid crowds and like a challenge, try fly fishing the North Fork of the Little Humboldt.

The river has a substantial populations of crayfish, caddisflies and mayflies. Damselflies are available near the beaver dams. In the fall grasshopper patterns bring explosive strikes.

The North Fork of the Little Humboldt River is the home of native Lahontan cutthroat trout.

East Fork Quinn River

The largest tributary of the Quinn River begins 7,240 feet up the east slope of the Santa Rosas. From the Humboldt National Forest to the Quinn River on the Fort McDermitt Indian Reservation the river runs 27 miles. Twenty-three of these miles lie inside Forest Service land.

Brown trout dominate the East Fork. The water also holds rainbow, brook and cutthroat trout. Speckled dace is the dominant forage fish. The browns reproduce naturally in this remote river, and behind the beaver dams can reach 20 inches.

Willows and meadow grass dominate the river in the accessible areas upstream of McDermitt. Approximately 10 miles of river flows through a steep canyon. Access is easiest upstream of the steep terrain.

If you've been fishing the North Fork of the Little Humboldt River, go north from Greely Crossing. A single lane dirt road forks to the southwest and leads to the upper East Fork. From U.S. 95 turn west just south of McDermitt at the fire station.

Fly fishing with short leaders and dry flies is very effective on the East Fork of the Quinn. High-floating dry flies like a Humpy fool a lot of fish. The stream has good numbers of mayflies, caddisflies and golden stoneflies. Damselflies hatch near the mazes of beaver dams. Also, fall fly fishermen carry a few grasshopper patterns.

Rainbow trout live in the East Fork of the Quinn River.

Chapter 3: Pershing County

The Humboldt Sink is really a shallow terminal lake for Nevada's longest river. Situated west of the ranching and mining community of Lovelock, the sink is easily visible from Interstate 80.

Around Lovelock is rich bottom land left by the receding ancient Lake Lahontan and irrigated by the Humboldt River. Emigrant wagon trains rested their stock nearby in what they called Big Meadow before crossing the 40 Mile Desert.

Rye Patch Reservoir is the biggest fishing hole for miles around and the key to today's ranching. Rye Patch is a phenomenal fishery, but also can suffer from prolonged drought like most of Nevada's fisheries. Humboldt River fishing in the area is supported by Rye Patch. Fish escape the reservoir over the spillway or swim up river to spawn.

Humboldt River

During the mass wagon migrations of the last century, the Humboldt River was a blessing soon reduced to a curse. The turbid water was a lifesaver after the deserts of western Utah and eastern Nevada. By the time the emigrants reached what would become Humboldt County, they had tired of its taste and smell.

As a fishery, this section of river is dependent on variable water flows. During the high-water years of the 1980s, walleye from Rye Patch Reservoir— roughly 40 river miles away—swam up to Winnemucca to spawn.

During the same time, largemouth bass and white crappie lived in the river up stream of Winnemucca to Golconda. In the oxbow areas of the meandering river, the bass and crappie found refuge among the hard stem bulrush and willows. That was a short term fishery. However, the local fisheries biologist believes it will return when the drought ends and water flows remain consistent. Even during bad flow years there can be some good catfishing in this section of the Humboldt River.

Access to the river is excellent in Winnemucca. Otherwise access to the river is from Interstate 80 interchanges. Expect improved dirt roads that get sloppy when the rain falls.

In the river below Rye Patch Reservoir local anglers catch walleye, bass, white bass-striped bass hybrids and trout. Foot access below the dam is good, but few anglers go very far downriver.

Rye Patch Reservoir

Considering the state record was broken three times in three weeks, it is easy to see walleye is king at Rye Patch. Before the reservoir draw down and resulting fish loss of 1992, seven- to 10-pound walleye were common. The reservoir still has that potential today.

Rye Patch covers 11,400 surface acres alongside Interstate 80, 23 miles east of Lovelock, Nevada at exit 129. The deepest part of the reservoir, at 67 feet, is near the dam, but the number doesn't tell the lake's story. The reservoir's upper end averages only 17 feet deep. True, the river channel is 30 feet deep, but it is a narrow corridor compared to the broad littoral zone of the upper lake. This makes for a tremendous fishery for largemouth bass and white crappie—when the reservoir is full.

Recovery from the latest drought offers anglers hope. When Rye Patch's level drops, bulrush, willows and tamarisk take root near the old river channel. As the water level rises after the drought, those plants recycle their nutrients into the fishery. Aquatic vegetation blooms and the fish respond. As an example, during fall of 1995, work on Rye Patch Dam necessitated a fish salvage operation in the Humboldt River below the reservoir. Fisheries workers recovered walleye in the 12- through 22-inch range.

Walleye fishing in the reservoir is good when there is water. However, many anglers prefer to try for them in the Humboldt River below the dam. The first mile of river sees most of the fishing pressure, but local anglers catch fish all the way down stream to Lovelock.

Trout planted since the 1992 fish loss now measuring 19 to 22 inches were moved back to the reservoir. Wipers, a white bass-striped bass hybrid, measuring 17 inches and in the four- and five-pound category, were recovered too.

A prolific and self-sustaining Rye Patch white bass fishery was lost to the 1992 draw down. A change in management strategy introduced the wipers as a larger and easier managed sport fish. Since the 1992 draw down, the Division of Wildlife has stocked Alabama spotted and northern largemouth bass. Both species are responding to the rapidly improving conditions. Largemouth bass constitute the second largest sport fish population according to gill net samples.

At one time the white crappie fishery at Rye Patch was the biggest sport fish in terms of numbers. They too were lost in 1992, but have been replaced with wipers.

The channel catfishing is phenomenal at Rye Patch. Fisheries biologist Jim French has checked catfish over 30 pounds. Catfish weighing six to seven pounds are common and fishermen regularly catch limits of 16- to 17-inch fish.

Rye Patch State Recreation Area has picnic, camping and boat launch facilities available for a fee. All of this is located near the dam at Interstate 80's exit

129. Access to the rest of the 26-mile-long reservoir is via dirt roads. A network of roads covers the northern and southern shorelines. The main roads ride high on bluffs overlooking the water and the feeder roads drop down to the water. A four-wheel-drive vehicle is a good idea even during dry weather. Occasional deep ruts, steep climbs and surprisingly soft sand will trap unprepared anglers.

At the Imlay interchange on the Interstate, an improved dirt road leads north and crosses the Humboldt River at Callahan Bridge. This is a good way to access the upper end of the reservoir when it is full.

CHAPTER 4: Douglas County

The fertile Carson Valley is the showcase of Douglas County. Nevada's first settlement, Genoa, sits at the base of the nearly vertical Sierra below Lake Tahoe. The forks of the Carson River met in this broad valley and agriculture is still a primary industry over a century later.

Though only four fishable waters are listed here, anglers will find many reasons to linger in this western Nevada county. Minden and Gardnerville are bustling centers of industry and offer everything fishermen can possibly need. Lake Tahoe lies within the county with its unique blend of alpine beauty and tourism. Farther south and still on the California-Nevada border is Topaz Reservoir a fishing destination for local and visiting anglers.

As for the fishing, Douglas County has much to tempt casual and fanatic anglers alike.

Spooner Lake

Nevada's only catch-and-release lake fishery is located 11 miles west of Carson City and just east of the intersection of Highways 50 and 28. Spooner Lake actually sits just inside the eastern rim of the Lake Tahoe Basin. Only 100 surface acres big and 22 feet deep, Spooner's water source is snow melt, springs and seeps.

The trout—rainbow, brown, tiger and cutthroat—bring the fishermen to this picturesque spot among tall pines. All the trout grow rapidly, but do not reproduce because of the lack of spawning streams. During 1993, the Division of Wildlife stocked 1,576 rainbow, 500 brown, 500 tiger and 124 cutthroat trout in Spooner. Brown trout feed on the lake's tui chubs and can reach the 18- to 20-inch range.

Because this lake is so shallow, bank fishing is not recommended. Thick growths of rooted aquatic weeds foul lures and flies. Instead, float tubes are the most popular way to get to the fish. If you want to bring a boat you can, but the parking lot is at least a quarter mile from the water. There is no boat launch facility at Spooner. Boats with motors are prohibited.

The catch-and-release restrictions at Spooner limit anglers to single hook, barbless lures and flies. A favorite technique for fly fishermen is to position their tube or boat at the edge of the aquatic weeds and fan out casts using leech and damsel patterns. Insect life includes mayflies, damsels, cased caddisflies, snails and leeches.

Spooner Lake access is through a state park. This is a day-use facility only and a $4 fee is charged. However, the facilities are well maintained including picnic tables, barbeques and flush toilets. Fishing reports are available from most Reno-Carson City area fishing and sporting goods stores.

Topaz Reservoir

Topaz Reservoir straddles the Nevada-California border approximately 37 miles south of Carson City alongside U.S. Highway 395. This is a big lake at the base of steep mountains. The lake covers 2,400 surface acres with its 3 1/2 mile length and 1 1/2 mile width. At its deepest, Topaz reaches 92 feet, but averages 52 feet deep.

During 1995 the lake received 14 rainbow trout plants totaling 83,333 fish from Nevada alone. Creel census revealed the catch averaged between 12 and 15 inches. The reservoir's record trout include a nine-pound, nine-ounce rainbow and a 12-pound brown. Other game fish in Topaz include bowcutt and tiger trout and bullhead catfish.

Boaters caught 76 percent of the fish according to the 1995 creel census. The reason is the lake's thermal stratification. During the last prolonged drought the layers of water temperature were pronounced. By fishing from a boat, trollers kept their lures and baits just above the thermocline or about 20 feet deep. Flashers followed by a worm-baited hook is the favored trolling rig. Topaz, however, has a good population of minnows. That is why minnow-imitating lures like floating Rapalas do so well. Shore fishermen did well early in the season, January and February, before the lake stratifies. Floating baits or inflated worms are preferred.

Spring is also the time for fly fishermen at Topaz. Trout working midge hatches in the shallows at the south end are within reach of sinking lines. Other insects active during the spring months include mayflies and damselflies.

Access along the steep western shore is limited. The Douglas County Park has good access along the north and northeast areas.

Because Topaz sits on the border, several resorts and restaurants sit on the hill above the water. Also a popular summer location for area residents of Carson City, Minden and Gardnerville, Topaz has a full-service marina and two improved public boat ramps. Camping is also available in public and private campgrounds.

Lake Tahoe

The highest lake in the United States also has the clearest water. The reason the water is so clear is the lake's thin littoral zone/food production shelf. Still, Lake Tahoe offers more than scenery, gaming and snow and water skiing. For anglers not easily intimidated by its size, Tahoe presents a unique fishing opportunity.

Lake Tahoe covers 193 square miles or 123,000 acres. The lake is 1,645 feet deep—deeper than the Carson Valley to the east. Tahoe holds 13 billion tons of water which is enough to cover California with over one foot of water. At maximum capacity, the lake's elevation is 6,229 feet.

Despite its size, and because of its location and altitude, Tahoe has a small forage base. But the lake produces some truly big fish. Nevada's Trophy Fish Program lists the following records for Lake Tahoe: rainbow trout: 9-pound, 4-ounce, 27 1/2-inch; brown trout: 12-pound, 29-inch; cutthroat trout: 12-pound 14-ounce, 31-inch; brook trout: 5-pound, 19-inch; mackinaw: 37-pound, 6-ounce, 44 inches; and kokanee salmon: 4-pound, 13-ounce, over 25 inches long.

Like Pyramid Lake, Tahoe's native fish is the Lahontan cutthroat. Also like Pyramid, Tahoe's cutthroat became extinct during the 1940s. Today Lake Tahoe's fishery is maintained as a combined effort of Nevada's Division of Wildlife and California's Department of Fish and Game.

Approximately 30 percent of the lake lies within Nevada. Most Nevada anglers work the waters between the Cave Rock boat ramp and Sand Harbor State Park boat ramp. During 1995, Nevada released 65,000 rainbow trout in the area between Cave Rock and Sand Harbor.

Creel checks by Nevada fisheries officials reveal three popular angling methods. Shore fishing, especially in the Cave Rock area, consistently produces fish. Fishermen can capture minnows from the lake to use as bait or cast lures. Fly tackle appears to be the neglected tackle at Tahoe. However Randy Johnson, a fly fishing guide from Truckee, California, has waded the shallow points of the lake in the evenings to intercept large trout feeding near the surface.

Top line trolling works best from May through September. No special tackle is needed, just the same rigs used in other trout lakes. Adding trolling weights, however, gives anglers better depth control. Again, trolling with fly tackle is a tactic not seen at Tahoe. Maybe fly fishermen don't feel comfortable casting and trolling on a lake 22 1/2-miles-long and 12 miles wide.

Tahoe is home to traditional deep line trolling tactics for mackinaw. Deep lining involves braided wire lines tipped with monofilament leaders, flashing blades and minnows fished as deep as 600 feet. Stiff action rods and reels capable of holding lots of line are a must. If you've never experienced this type of fishing and would like to try, several Tahoe guides offer half-day trips.

Jigging is another Tahoe mackinaw tactic. Drifting on a calm lake, jigs or minnow-baited hooks are lowered to the bottom. Two or three cranks on the reel raises the bait above the flat bottom. Now raise and lower the rod two to four feet at a time. Keep in touch with the bait on the way down or you'll miss most of the strikes.

Lake Tahoe is a tourist destination. Whether on the Nevada side with its gaming or the California side, the lake is virtually ringed with hotels and restaurants.

Anglers will have little trouble finding accommodations, but may flinch at some of the prices. Reno and Carson City, however, are just 30 minutes away.

Carson River

The headwaters of the Carson River begin above the 10,000-foot elevation in the Sierra Nevada Mountains of California. The East and West Forks join near the historic pioneer settlement of Genoa. The West Fork closely follows Highways 88 and 89 in California. Highways 4 and 89 parallel the East Fork for a short distance near Markleeville, also in California. In Nevada most of this river system is isolated except near Minden and Gardnerville and Carson City. Downstream from Carson, U.S.

The orchestra is ready to begin. Each rod is fished at different depths.

Highway 50 comes close to the river as it flows into Lahontan Reservoir.

A health advisory for the river below Dayton to Lahontan Reservoir is in effect. During the boom days of the Comstock Lode and Virginia City's glory, mercury was used to separate gold and silver from raw ore. Much of that mercury is still in the river system.

The best fishing, according to creel census, is the Rhenstroth Dam and the golf course areas of Gardnerville. East of downtown Carson City try the area from Mexican Dam downstream to Spring Hole. Continuing downstream, anglers like to fish at Ellis, Dayton Bridge and two access points along Fort Churchill Road.

Below Mexican Dam anglers find largemouth and smallmouth bass and trout. Most trout, however, reside above this dam. Also below Mexican Dam crayfish become an important food source. In addition, anglers will find green sunfish, black bullhead catfish and carp.

The Carson River flows close to main traffic arteries along the eastern Sierra. As a result, anglers will find accommodations of all types along the way. Most camping opportunities, however, exist along the lower reaches near Fort Churchill and at Lahontan Reservoir.

CHAPTER 5: Carson City

Nevada's capital city is named after the legendary scout and mountain man Kit Carson. The county bears the same name. Initially confusing for some visitors they soon adapt when they realize that Carson City is the smallest county in the state. As a result, the county has few places to fish. The Carson River, for example, is described in Chapter 4 under Douglas County though it flows through Carson City and Lyon County.

Carson City does have something for anglers besides politics and tourism, however. Hobart Reservoir is the county's claim to angling fame, but the Carson also lies along the major U.S. Highways 50 and 395.

Hobart Reservoir

Originally built in 1877 to store water for Virginia City, this little reservoir is a picturesque fishery. Only 10 surface acres big and a mere 15 feet deep, Hobart sits above Carson City at the 7,524-foot elevation. The surrounding red fir, quaking aspen, willow, Jeffrey pine, lodgepole pine and mountain alder make this spot a must on the angler's list.

Hobart's access is limited to hikers. From Lake View Hill, 30 miles south of Reno and 10 miles from Carson City, it is a five-mile walk from the locked gate. This is the long way and mostly up hill. From Carson City's Ash Canyon Road and a four-wheel-drive, the hike is 1 1/4 miles from the trail head. When Nevadan's say four-wheel-drive, they mean crawling speed and a short wheel base.

Hobart backs up two streams. Both creeks are small, but their inlets are marshy areas inundated with beaver dams—perfect brook trout water. The reservoir first opened to fishing in 1981. In 1988 rainbow trout were introduced to supplement the lake's brook trout. During 1994, 53 cutthroat trout from Marlette Lake were moved to Hobart. That same year saw 1,001 Eagle Lake rainbow and 500 bowcuts planted too. Creel census data collected for 10 days during the 1994 season shows 263 trout taken by 89 anglers. The size ranged from 3 to 14 inches, but the Marlette cutthroat can reach 20 inches. Ten year data shows anglers catching 4.36 fish per day between 1983 and 1992.

All but the deepest part of the reservoir is covered with thick growths of aquatic plants. Some grow as tall as 10 feet. This is perfect habitat for the insects that trout feed on. Mayfly nymphs, damsel nymphs, midges, scuds and caddisflies are all abundant.

Lure fishermen find their favorite hardware works well at Hobart. Match the lure size to the size of the fish.

Fly fishermen that like dry-fly action can work the midge and mayfly hatches. Nymphs fished inches below the surface are deadly. Woolly Buggers and leeches on intermediate sinking lines are also a favorite. Big trout prefer the deep water near the dam during midday, so go deep when fishing there.

Float tubes make the reservoir more accessible than wading. A tube is easily carried like a backpack and doesn't weigh much. Waders and fins are also a good idea and don't forget to bring your lunch, insect repellent and sunscreen. Please carry out all of your trash.

Anglers may be tempted to spend a night along the banks of this high-country fishery, but camping is not permitted. Fire rings near the Ash Canyon trailhead mean others have camped there, but driving back is a better idea. A wild fire here could ruin the scenery and the fishing.

Look to the Reno sporting goods stores for Hobart Reservoir fishing reports.

CHAPTER 6: Lyon County

Lyon County holds a lot of fishing opportunities. Rivers flowing through this county include the Carson (Chapter 4) and the Walker (Chapter 6). Reservoirs in the county, however, are limited.

Mason Valley Wildlife Management Area and half of Lahontan Reservoir constitute most of Lyon county's still-water fishing. Mason Valley is just north of Yerington. Lahontan is east of Carson City alongside U.S. Highway 50.

Services for anglers within Lyon County are limited. The primary businesses are agriculture and mining. Around Yerington, anglers will find most of the services they need. Also, Lahontan Reservoir is a major Nevada recreational area so look for service at Silver Springs.

Walker River

Like the Carson River, both branches of the Walker River originate high in the Sierra Nevada Mountains. The East Fork travels through 52 miles of Nevada before meeting the West Fork in Mason Valley. Public access to the East Fork is limited.

On the East Fork of the Walker River, the Sceirine Ranch along Nevada Highway 182 at the Nevada-California border allows fishing access to about a mile of stream. Downstream is seven miles of the previously private fishery called the Rosaschi Ranch. What was the Rosaschi Ranch is now under U.S. Forest Service control, and, as of this writing, land use plans are in development. Nevada has placed catch-and-release regulations on this seven miles of the East Fork. The next public access is the Elbow and Racoon Beach. Both are reached via improved dirt road passable by two-wheel-drive vehicles during good weather. There is no overnight camping in the Elbow area.

West Fork public access is also limited. This branch of the Walker in Nevada technically begins at Topaz Canal, a diversion canal below Topaz Resevoir. The canal's steep banks discourage most anglers, but at times the fishing here is excellent. Downstream anglers can get to the water at Hoye Canyon, Wilson Canyon rest area and in Wilson Canyon. This area is a picturesque agricultural region along Nevada Highway 208 and the road passes through Wellington and Smith Valley. Camping is permitted in the Hoye Canyon and Wilson Canyon areas.

Brown trout, rainbow trout and Rocky Mountain whitefish live in the Walker River system. Occasionally a largemouth bass is landed too. Nevada's Division of

Dale Rasaschi prepares to release a fat rainbow that lives on his East Walker River ranch.

Wildlife 1993 population survey estimated between 2,000 and 5,000 brown trout per mile in the East Fork. That is a lot of good fishing by most anglers' definition. Still more browns and rainbows were stocked in both forks during 1993.

Willows line the banks of both forks. At times the willows become so thick that the only way to fish the river is to wade. Suspended silt discolors the water in the Walker River, but doesn't affect the fishing. All the traditional tackle—bait, lures and flies—catch fish. Fly fishermen can expect to see caddisflies, stoneflies, mayflies, damselflies, midges, scuds, black flies and minnows.

Mason Valley Wildlife Management Area

In 1955 the State of Nevada purchased 8,500 acres of ranch land and turned it into Mason Valley Wildlife Management Area. Today the property totals over 13,000 acres. This is primarily a waterfowl management area, but the habitat also supports deer, quail, pheasant, turkeys, geese, dove and fish.

Only the four western ponds are open to angling. All four ponds are shallow wetlands created by dikes built along natural drainage channels. The primary water source for these impounds are the underground wells that support the Mason Valley Fish Hatchery. The water is cold enough to support trout year-round and warm enough for bass, bluegill, crappie and catfish.

Hinkson Slough

The first water below the hatchery is Hinkson Slough. Hinkson's water is rich in aquatic life—plant and animal—and the trout grow as much as one inch per month. Trout don't reproduce naturally at Hinkson due to the lack of a stream, but they can reach sizes of up to nine pounds or more.

Bass reproduce in the shallows. The average largemouth measured 12 3/4 inches in 1993, but 2- to 5-pound largemouth are landed every year.

Hinkson Slough owes its rich water to the hatchery. Algae blooms clog the channels late in the year, but the trout and bass are still there. They feed all year on leeches, water boatmen, mayflies, damselflies, dragonflies and midges. Surface-feeding fish can make Hinkson Slough look as though it is raining under a cloudless sky.

The next pond below Hinkson is Bass Pond. Another cattail- and tule-lined pond, Bass Pond has earned its name. There is ideal cover here for warm-water fish.

Crappie Pond also has good cover for bass, bluegill and crappie. The only thing missing as of this writing is water. Bass and Crappie ponds are dry as Nevada prepares to build a new 190-surface-acre fishing opportunity. If everything goes according to plan, North Pond should be available to anglers sometime in 1996. North Pond will have the same species of fish as Hinkson, with the addition of catfish.

The Division of Wildlife's strategy at Mason Valley is to manage Hinkson as a trophy fishery. Bass, Crappie and North Ponds will be managed under general fishing guidelines. Together the four ponds offer something for every angler.

Boating is allowed, but speed limit and flat wake rules are enforced. Fishing from a float tube is a tactic favored by fly fishermen and spin fishermen alike. The water temperatures, however, get very cold at the beginning of the season. Wear long underwear or the like in February through early April.

Mason Valley ponds for anglers: Hinkson Slough, Bass and Crappie ponds, and soon North Pond.

Mason Valley Wildlife Area is east of Alternate U.S. Highway 95 some 70 miles southeast of Reno, or 15 miles north of Yerington. Fishermen can get to the Wildlife Area via Miller Lane from the south or Sierra Way from the north. Both roads are well marked.

Camping at Mason Valley Wildlife Area is allowed between the hatchery and the Wildlife Area offices. A portable toilet is the only facility provided, so bring everything you need, including shade.

Mason Valley is an hour-and-a-half drive from Reno where full accommodations are available. Also the agricultural and mining community of Yerington to the south has hotels and restaurants.

Midges or chironomids swim by wiggling. They don't have legs or other appendages for movement.

Fort Churchill Cooling Ponds

Constructed as a cooling source for a steam generating plant, Fort Churchill Cooling Ponds is a Lyon County warm-water fishery. The plant sits near the East Walker River and along the northern boundary of the Mason Valley Wildlife Area.

Fishing at the ponds is by agreement between Sierra Pacific Power Company and the Nevada Division of Wildlife. Warm water from the plant enters the north end, east of the center dike. The water circulates south then west and north as it cools before re-entering the power plant. The ponds total 210 surface acres and average between 14 1/2 to 7 feet deep.

Leave the boats and float tubes home. Anglers can only cast from the outer dike. Access to the Cooling Ponds is via Mason Valley Wildlife Area along the southern dike. Wading is also forbidden. The center dike and other posted areas are closed to foot traffic too. There is a parking area with portable toilets, but no camping is allowed.

Lures, plastic worms and bait are the preferred tactics for the Cooling Ponds. Some fly fishermen are beginning to discover the Cooling Ponds too. Traditional trout fly tackle and streamer patterns can catch fish all season long.

During 1993, Wildlife officials checked 155 largemouth bass that averaged 13 3/4 inches. The biggest was 20 1/4 inches. In 1995, rumor of a 14-pound bass was unconfirmed, but a 9-pounder was checked. Channel catfish also live in this water. Again in 1993, 54 fish averaged 10 1/4 inches, with the biggest reaching 16 3/4 inches.

Naturally-spawned fish use the Cooling Pond's weeds for cover. Algae grows in the sheltered corners of the pond. The power plant circulates up to 98,400 gallons of water per minute when all units are operating. This creates a good current that anglers need to deal with. Water quality looks poor from a distance. Though you cannot see far into the ponds, the fish don't appear to mind.

Desert Creek

The only popular stream on the Nevada side of the Sweet Water Mountains is Desert Creek. A surprising fact considering the range has peaks

Ephemerella glacialis Super Crawler Western Green Drake with Hare's Ear.

over 10,000 feet tall. This range of mountains regularly has a thick mantle of snow every winter, even during dry years.

Desert Creek originates on the east flank of the Sweet Water Range at 8,700 feet where the East Fork joins the main fork. On the California side of the mountains, Lobdell Lake and its tributaries form the stream's headwaters. The creek is fishable from its origin for 18 miles down stream to the 5,800-foot elevation. From here water is diverted for irrigation.

Access to Desert Creek is excellent. Take Nevada Highway 338 south of Nevada 208 at the ranching community of Wellington. Four miles from Wellington look for a brown Forest Service sign pointing out the road leading west. A two-wheel-drive road parallels the stream from Nevada 338 to the 7,040-foot elevation. From this point a four-wheel drive road continues up toward Lobdell Lake.

At its lower elevations, Desert Creek's banks have thick stands of willows and sagebrush. In the narrow portions of the canyon getting to the water is difficult due to the vegetation. Farther up, the creek courses through meadows making for easier fishing. The road does cross the creek as it works up the mountains.

Fly fishermen will be pleased with the abundant insect hatches on Desert Creek. Stream surveys have identified the following insects: caddisflies, spotted sedge, stoneflies, little brown stones and golden stones; mayflies, green drakes, pale morning duns and blue-wing olives. Also water beetles and black flies are present in the stream. Big bite food is available in the form of sculpins.

During a 1979 stream survey, fisheries biologists estimated Desert Creek has 605 trout per mile. Brook, brown and rainbow trout inhabit the stream. Not all the trout are big, but rainbow trout are stocked regularly in the creek. Desert Creek was stocked with 6,200 rainbow trout over 10 inches long in 1995. The only Arctic grayling ever taken in Nevada was from Desert Creek. This rare fish came from Lobdell Lake where a small population of grayling live. Some locals believe the grayling was in reality caught across the California line, but who can tell where political boundaries are among the sagebrush and pines?

Camping is available in various places along the stream. At lower elevations, anglers may want to camp under cottonwoods and scrub pines like pinon and ponderosa pine. Farther up the mountain aspen and Jeffrey pine provide shade. All camping is primitive, however and anglers should come prepared. Some supplies are available in Wellington and Smith.

Fire danger increases as spring becomes summer. Rings of rocks mark old campfires, but open fires are not a good idea if they can be avoided.

CHAPTER 7: Churchill County

The agricultural center of the Silver State is probably Lahontan Valley and Fallon. The nation's first Reclamation Project, the Newlands Project, was intended to make this desert valley bloom.

Lahontan Reservoir was built by backing up the Carson River east of Fallon and diverting Truckee River water from Pyramid Lake to Lahontan. Farming has done well when prolonged droughts haven't interfered. In fact, the area is famous for its heart of gold cantaloupe.

East of Fallon is a series of desert terminal basins for the Carson River. Each has proven a vital waterfowl stop along the Pacific Fly Way. Also east of Fallon are training and bombing ranges for one of the Navy's biggest inland bases. Fallon Naval Air Station is an important part of the county.

Fallon is a city of hard-working, honest people. All services are available to anglers, but we always want more fishing tackle stores.

Indian Lakes/Stillwater Marsh

Indian Lakes is five fishable waters that total 549 surface acres. The water, however, is shallow and turbid. As a result, there is a lack of aquatic plants and insects. Agricultural return flow makes up the only water supply for Indian Lakes. This area is directly impacted by lower than normal snow packs in the Sierras. During prolonged droughts, little if any water will enter the area.

Still the Division of Wildlife tries to maintain a warm-water fishery when conditions permit. Predatory largemouth bass and black bullhead catfish are planted because they feed on the non-game fish in the lakes.

Statistics from 1992 show 228 anglers spent 947 days fishing Indian Lakes and Stillwater Marsh. They caught 1,230 fish. These numbers are down nearly 50 percent from 1991, but this data was collected during a prolonged drought.

Indian Lakes are located northeast of Fallon. From US Highway 95 north of Fallon look for the sign marking the turn to the east. The road is a combination of blacktop and graded gravel surface.

Lahontan Reservoir

Anglers living in Fallon and Fernley have a secret. For years they tried to keep the walleye fishing quiet, but now equally aggressive white bass fishing

The 1993 walleye spawn led to the largest age class of the warm-water predators in Lahontan to date.

is taking off. Add the white bass-striped bass hybrid called the wiper and the water skiers and swimmers at Lahontan Reservoir will begin sharing the water with more fishermen.

A rapid-growing predator, the walleye is a warm-water fish that was introduced into Lahontan Reservoir about 19 years ago. The biggest fish fishery officials netted in 1994 weighed 15 pounds. The big fish in 1993 came in at 12 1/2 pounds.

Another minnow-eating predator in Lahontan is the white bass and wiper. White bass spawn after the walleye along the sandy beaches the lake is famous for. Sandals, shorts and sunblock make this type of fishing a pleasant change from typical June fishing. Wipers grow bigger and faster than white bass. Lahontan has some old and big white bass that reach the 15-inch mark. The wipers, however, are averaging closer to 15 inches and about 2 1/4-pounds.

Some fly fishermen report catching up to 75 bass and walleyes in an evening. The best time to find the fish is between 4 o'clock and sunset. At dark the fish stop biting.

Streamers are effective and their size is not important. White and yellow are the favorite colors and occasionally chartreuse. These colors likely resemble the small forage fish available in Lahontan and are easily seen in the slightly murky water.

Other Lahontan reservoir game fish includes channel catfish, white catfish, white crappie, yellow perch and largemouth bass. Also, rainbow trout are stocked in the reservoir, but they don't do well during low-water years. The walleye, largemouth and wipers are supplemented by state stocking operations.

Lahontan is a moderately turbid man-made reservoir. The reservoir covers 15,000 acres south of U.S. Highway 50 and between Alternate U.S. 95 and Fallon, and lies within the boundaries of Lahontan State Park. Fees are charged for day-use, camping and boat launching. Improved boat ramps are available near the dam just off U.S. 50 and on the west end from Alternate U.S. 95.

Good fishing is found all around the lake if you have a boat. Roads are limited along the southern bank. Still, there is plenty of beach to cover. Look for rocky shorelines that meet sandy beaches. Also, submerged willows and cottonwood trees provide cover for the minnows the big predators are looking for.

Services and stores are available at Silver Springs at the intersection of U.S. 50 and Alternate 95. Fallon is 30 minutes to the east and Carson City another 30 minutes to the west.

CHAPTER 8: Mineral County

At first glance Mineral County does not seem to hold much for Nevada anglers. The county borders the southwestern edge of the Lahontan Basin where low desert hills find barely enough water to support sagebrush. All the streams seem to disappear into parched sand-filled arroyos and washes.

Yet in the northwest corner of the county lies the second most important cutthroat trout fishery in the state. Walker Lake, a smaller version of its sister Pyramid Lake, has supported continuous cutthroat fishing longer than Pyramid.

Hawthorne is the county's principle center of civilization. It is truly high desert community supported by a huge military munitions depot and gaming. Mining has increased in economic importance during the last decade.

Traveling fishermen will find all the services they need in Hawthorne. Everything from tackle to fishing reports, and hotels and restaurants are within minutes of Walker Lake's shores. The major blacktop road is U.S. Highway 95 that runs north to south, from Fallon south through Hawthorne and on to Las Vegas.

Walker Lake

A smaller version of Pyramid Lake, Walker Lake is smaller, but still has native cutthroat trout. In fact, Walker's cutthroat provided brood stock to re-establish cutthroat in Pyramid Lake during the 1950s. Today [1996] it is Pyramid Lake helping to maintain Walker Lake's trout.

U.S. Highway 95 runs along Walker Lake's western shore 72 miles south of Fallon and five miles north of Hawthorne, Nevada. The lake is 17 miles long, 6 1/2 miles wide and 140 feet deep. Like Pyramid, Walker's water is so alkaline or saline that only Lahontan cutthroat trout can survive. The lake's biggest cutt, according to the record book, weighed 14 pounds, 4 ounces and measured 34 inches. During 1993, however, the average sized trout measured 14 1/2 inches. Why the difference? Walker Lake's water is diverted for irrigation nearly the entire length of the Walker River and at both of its forks. Most of the river's water rights were divided up over a century ago. Walker Lake, on the other hand, did not receive water rights until 1979. As a result, the lake's level has dropped 110 feet since 1927.

Nevada anglers have not given up on Walker Lake. In fact, just the opposite is true. Mineral County's Chamber of Commerce hosts an annual Walker Lake Fishing Derby that lasts three days. Nevada's Division of Wildlife is also working hard to keep the lake a healthy and productive trout fishery.

Starting in 1995, fishery officials received help from the Pyramid Lake Indian Tribe. Cutthroat hatched in the Federal facility near Gardnerville were taken to Pyramid where they spent several days in holding pens. Once adjusted to the saline Pyramid water, the trout moved to Walker Lake. As a result the 5- and 6-inch fish planted in the spring of 1995 almost doubled in size by November.

Again, like Pyramid, Walker Lake's cutthroat grow quickly because they feed almost exclusively on minnows when chub production is good. Walker's water rose a good four feet as a result of the near record 1994-1995 winter. The fresh-water helped the tui chub spawn and the trout fishing rebounded.

Traditional tactics for boaters include trolling number 3 Torpedo spoons. The favorite color is green with black spots. Also, some fishermen use Flat Fish. Later, as the lake's water temperature drops, Rebel lures imitating crawdads become popular. Trollers work from 40 feet deep to 20 feet. Downriggers and Dipsy Divers help get lures down to the trout.

Fly fishermen find good fishing in Walker Lake too. The north and east sides of the lake offer the best fly fishing. Twenty Mile Beach, Sand Point and Old Ski Beach are popular fly fishing spots. Access is limited to boats or four-wheel-drive vehicles. Soft blow sand along the east side of Walker Lake can trap the best off-road trucks.

Fly fishermen use Pyramid Lake rigs with black Woolly Worms with red egg sacks and shooting head lines. Pyramid fly anglers began using two-fly casts about a decade ago. Now a bright fly dropper and a dark tip fly is considered standard at Pyramid.

When weather permits, fly fishermen are willing to launch float tubes at Walker Lake. Like Pyramid, Walker fishes best during cold weather months so hypothermia is an issue wading or float tubing anglers must consider.

Two improved boat ramps give Walker anglers easy access. Sportsman's Beach has the newest and best facility and is located just off Highway 95 north of the Cliffs. A small state park south of the Cliffs has the other boat ramp.

Camping in primitive facilities is provided near both ramps. In Hawthorne anglers can find hotels, restaurants and a well-stocked tackle store.

Facing Page: A great blue heron surveys for a fish dinner.

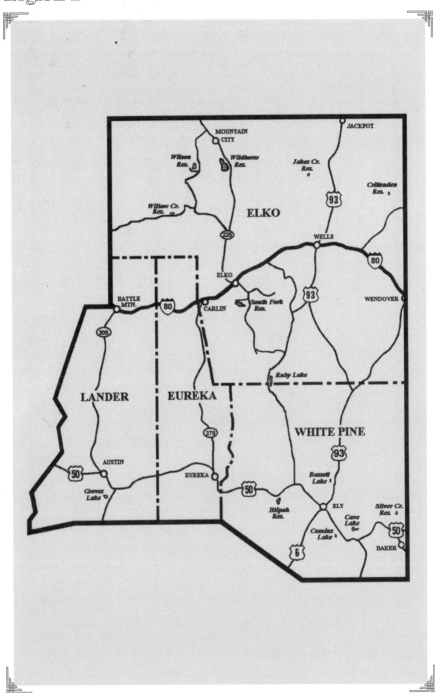

Region 2

The northeast corner of Nevada, Region 2, receives the most moisture. During good water years, the mountains keep their snow caps into July and August, or beyond. As a result, these four counties have more fishing than the other two regions. Eureka is the only county not listed here.

In this section anglers will find six mountain ranges and their small streams. For one of those mountain ranges, the Rubys, I give a description of its alpine lakes.

Major cities include Elko and Ely. Anglers will find all services, including tackle, in both communities. Interstate 80 and U.S. Highway 50 are the main east-to-west roads. U.S. Highway 93 is the main north-to-south route.

Nevada's longest river, the Humboldt, begins in Elko County and flows west into the desert of Pershing County. The forks of the Owyhee and Jarbidge flow north into the Snake River of Idaho. From White Pine County, the White River historically flowed south to the Colorado River—today it is an intermittent dry channel.

Ranching and mining dominate the region's economy. Occasionally, the wandering fisherman will need permission to cross private land. Most of these waters, however, are accessible.

Put it all together and Nevada anglers can spend a lot of time fishing the waters of Region 2.

CHAPTER 9: Elko County

Talk about fishable water in Nevada and most anglers look to the northeast corner of the state. Sitting there on both the Idaho and Utah borders is Elko County.

In addition to having more places to fish than any other county in the state, Elko holds claim to some of the state's best hunting. Whether fishing, hunting, hiking or camping, this county has something for every outdoorsman.

The largest community is Elko. The city has grown rapidly the last decade or so with Nevada's newest mining boom. Some of the richest gold mines in the state are in Elko County.

Wells is another important community. A major stop along the freeway, Wells also marks the intersection of U.S. Highway 93, an important road for Nevada anglers.

Not all of the fishable waters of Elko County are described here. The major

Old mines and mining equipment dot the mountains where Nevada anglers travel.

ones are, however. There is enough here to get your attention and make you want to explore this corner of the Silver State.

Wild Horse Reservoir

Winters get so cold at this northern Elko County reservoir that area weathermen use it as a thermometer. In fact, between November and April the ice on Wild Horse reaches 16 to 20 inches thick. Is this a good place for ice fishing? You bet, but that's not all.

The headwaters of the East Fork of the Owyhee River and a few creeks feed the reservoir. South, just over a low ridge, is the upper reaches of the North Fork of the Humboldt River. Both rivers originate on the east flank of the Independence Mountains and roughly follow Nevada Highway 225. The Owyhee flows north and the Humboldt goes south.

Wild Horse is consistently among the most fished reservoirs in the state. Ask a stranger if they've heard of the lake. If they haven't, they just arrived in Nevada.

At 2,380 surface acres when full, this irrigation reservoir holds plenty of angling opportunities. The water is rich in nutrients that support aquatic life. Fisheries biologists have recorded growth rates of as much as 1.1 inches per month. Algae blooms spoil the surface late in the summer until the first frost of fall, but it is only a temporary annoyance.

Since a 1988 rough fish eradication, only rainbow, brown and hybrid bow-cut trout have been seen. Some brook trout and wild cutthroat live in the tributary streams and could reach the reservoir. The lake grows rainbows up to 8 pounds, browns over 12 pounds.

The warm-water fishery in Wild Horse includes smallmouth bass, white crappie and channel catfish. Like South Fork Reservoir, the bass are used as a biological control for rough fish.

Tactics for Wild Horse typically involve trolling lures or bait. Shore anglers cast bait rigs near drop-offs. Recently, fly fishing has begun to catch on at Wild Horse. From a boat or an inflatable such as a float tube, fly fishermen can work the productive shallows along the west and northern shoreline.

Wild Horse State Park is located 65 miles north of Elko via Nevada Highway 225. The park has full-facility camping. An improved boat ramp is also available whether you camp or not.

Access from Highway 225 along the reservoir's eastern shore is excellent. Some areas, however, are controlled by the Sho-Pai Tribe and they charge a daily fee. The tribe also allows primitive camping. West of Highway 225 near the dam is a Bureau of Land Management campground. This facility does not have direct access to the water.

Driving in from the south, look for Archie's Wildhorse Ranch & Resort on the right. Across the highway is an informal settlement of houses and mobile homes. Work your way among the homes to reach the western shore of the reservoir. Be careful, however. When dry the road is rutted and rough. When wet or when the lake is near capacity, it is muddy, hence the deep ruts.

East Fork Owyhee River

Sometimes, the obvious is easily missed. The East Fork of the Owyhee River is a good example.

A tailwater fishery, the East Fork flows north from Wild Horse Reservoir. As the river cuts through a moderately steep canyon, Nevada Highway 225 parallels the stream for roughly six miles. What discourages most anglers, however, is the lack of pull-outs and thick stands of willows and trees along the banks.

In a sense, these obstacles preserve the fishery. Only the determined angler willing and prepared to wade right up the middle of the river will truly work the water. Casual fishermen work pools and runs near the turn-offs or close to Wild Horse Crossing Campground, but aren't prepared to work the rest of the river.

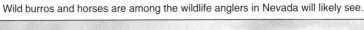

Wild burros and horses are among the wildlife anglers in Nevada will likely see.

Where the river leaves the canyon, private land ownership begins. From here to the community of Mountain City access is limited. After leaving Mountain City the river crosses into the Duck Valley Indian Reservation. While the Sho-Pai Tribe will likely sell fishermen a license to fish the river (see Sheep Creek Reservoir), few fishermen work the river.

The East Fork of the Owyhee River is underfished. Creel census checks by fisheries officials range from a high of 35 anglers to a low of eight anglers per year. Fishing, however, was good for those fishermen. Anglers averaged two fish each and the size of the trout averaged 12 1/2 to 14 inches. The biggest fish, a brown trout, measured 15 inches. During the fall of 1995, this writer averaged seven rainbows and browns per hour and the smallest was roughly 12 inches long.

Below Wildhorse Reservoir, the East Fork of the Owyhee River is a brushy, must-wade stream.

Sheep Creek Reservoir

Located totally within the Duck Valley Indian Reservation, Sheep Creek draws Idaho and Nevada anglers. This is big fish water that is open to all types of tackle, but is very popular with fly fishermen.

North of Wild Horse Reservoir and 12 miles west of Highway 225 is where to look for this productive reservoir. Sheep Creek Reservoir has 1,000 surface acres of water, but is only 22 feet deep. This broad littoral zone provides plenty of food for the lake's fast-growing trout.

Fly fishing is popular according to Melvin Blossom the tribe's game warden. Blossom is the best available source for fishing reports. He visits anglers as much as twice a day collecting fishing and camping fees and fishing reports.

Sheep Creek's Eagle Lake and Kamloops rainbow trout like big bites. Typically the smaller fish key in on the midges, mayflies and scuds. The bigger trout, those that reach the 15-pound-plus size, prefer Woolly Buggers, Sheep Creek Specials, Stayner Streamers and Mohair leech patterns.

Rainbow trout, stocked by the Sho-Pai Tribe live in Sheep Creek Reservoir.

Bait fishing and trolling lures is permitted, but fly fishing accounts for most of the trout landed. Even trollers use flies when their lures fail to produce.

The tribe buys and stocks trout from fingerling size up to 15 pounds. There is no minimum size limit.

The reservoir has 32 covered campsites with picnic tables spread around two thirds of the shoreline. A boat ramp with a floating dock is available near the southwest end to the lake. Access is via paved and improved dirt roads from Owyhee on Nevada State Route 11. There is also a dirt airstrip for fly-in anglers.

The Sho-Pai Tribe charges for fishing and camping. Fishing permits cost $5 for one day, $9 for two days, or $4 for three or more days. Camping is $3 per night.

Anglers should be prepared for weather. Here, near the Idaho-Nevada border, Gulf of Alaska storms can impact the fishing. During spring and fall, conditions can change quickly so come equipped.

The reservoir's north shore butts up against a lava rock plateau with a steep rimrock border. Access is available along most of the kidney-shaped reservoir. Expect rutted roads early in the spring and sloppy road conditions during wet weather.

Dry Creek Reservoir

Twenty-four and a half miles southwest of Owyhee and 1 1/2 miles west of Nevada Route 11 is Dry Creek Reservoir. Few cars traveling the improved gravel road notice the reservoir. When southbound, the driver must look back over his shoulder. Northbound traffic can catch a quick glimpse if they pay attention.

If you get the idea this 109 surface acre, 40-foot deep reservoir gets overlooked, you are right. Especially in late summer and fall when irrigation draws the reservoir down to under half its capacity. Don't be fooled, however. Many Elko County anglers try to keep this water secret because it produces good trout and bass fishing regularly.

The trout fishery is relatively young at Dry Creek. Trout were first stocked in 1963 and smallmouth bass in 1974. There are largemouth here too. According to Division of Wildlife records, brown trout also live in the lake, or have. But Dry Creek Reservoir's entry in the Nevada Trophy Fish Program is for a 18-1/4-inch, 4-pound 3-ounce smallmouth bass taken in 1991. During 1993, creel checks showed the rainbows averaged 13 inches in length.

Expect seasonal algal blooms and turbid waters from spring runoff. The fish and the insects, however, don't seem to mind. About half the reservoir is under 25 feet deep (when full), which provides the game fish a smorgasbord of food. The lake is home to mayflies, damselflies, dragonflies, snails, water boatmen, scuds, crayfish and rough fish.

The land around the reservoir is privately owned, but public access is allowed. Float tubes, inflatable boats and small car-top-craft can launch just about anywhere the road reaches the water. Boats on trailers may have a difficult time launching.

Camping is permitted as witnessed by fire rings around points of land above the high-water mark. Conditions are primitive, however. High clearance two-wheel-drive vehicles can negotiate the last 1 1/5 miles of road. Motorhomes and large trailers will have a difficult time getting through the steep washes.

Wilson (Sink) Reservoir

Wilson is another well known Nevada reservoir. The 800-surface-acre lake is managed as a quality put-grow-and-take fishery. Nevada's Division of Wildlife says Wilson rainbows average 13 inches. The reservoir, however, has produced brown trout weighing over 11 pounds. Wilson is also home to largemouth bass. The fact that 83 percent of the lake is 15 feet deep or less means plenty of bass cover. While a 13-inch bass is considered average, the reservoir has produced largemouth over 7 pounds.

The shallow water also means thick mats of rooted weeds can make bank fishing frustrating in summer months. There is a concrete boat ramp available

A Wilson (Sink) Reservoir rainbow—bigger trout do live in this Elko County Reservoir.

for a $1 fee. Car-top boats and float tubes can launch almost anywhere there is public access, if they don't mind the weeds.

Most of the lake is on BLM land, but 2 1/2 acres is private land. Shore access is basically limited to the area around the spillway north to the dam on the west bank. From the boat ramp north to the dam, the terrain is sheer rock cliffs.

At different times fish key on damselflies, dragonflies, mayflies or midge hatches. Occasionally, the trout decide to concentrate on large snails seen drifting in the waves.

The Bureau of Land Management has a developed campground along the western shore of Wilson Reservoir. They provide vault toilets, picnic tables, barbecue stands and water.

Getting to the water is limited along the north and northeast portions of the reservoir. The road leading to Wilson crosses the reservoir's spillway before turning north into the Wilson Reservoir Recreation Area.

Bull Run Reservoir

A 1990 agreement with private landowners limited access to walk-in traffic. The idea was to develop a trophy fishery along the west slope of the Independence Mountains. For various reasons, the trophy fishery did not develop.

Nevada's Division of Wildlife changed the reservoir back to general regulations beginning in 1996.

Fishing at Bull Run has been open to the public since the 120-surface-acre reservoir was built in 1954. Historically, upstream wild trout populations moved into the lake and were augmented by stocking. A drought in 1991 dried up the reservoir. The reservoir has not been stocked since and only wild brook and redband trout drifting downstream live there as of this writing. Bull Run, however, is a popular Elko County fishery.

Food sources for trout include typical lake living insects. Also, there is a good population of scuds and snails in the reservoir. Good news for fly fishermen is the relative lack of rooted aquatic vegetation.

Bull Run Reservoir is located north of Nevada Highway 226 and one mile east of the Maggie Summit Road. Look for a large green sign with white lettering about 65 miles north of Elko. The dam backs up Bull Run Creek at the western end of Bull Run Basin to form a bathtub-shaped reservoir. Walk-in access is from the Maggie Summit road and is about a one mile hike. Ideal for backpacking-in a float tube, the walk eliminates boats.

The landowner has provided a wide turn-out from the graded dirt road for camping. Plan on bringing everything with you if you camp and don't be surprised if the rancher's cattle stop by to visit.

Independence Mountains

The Independence Mountains are encircled by the Duck Valley Indian Reservation on the North, Nevada Highway 225 on the east and Nevada Highway 226 on the south and west. Add the Maggie Summit Road running over the ridge between Mountain City and Bull Run Basin and fishermen find a road system providing good access to several streams.

Most of the streams are accessible with two-wheel-drive. If you cannot drive to the water, then foot and horseback access is available.

Badger Creek

Badger Creek flows into the East Fork of the Owyhee River below Wild Horse Reservoir. Access is by foot or, with landowner permission, by four-wheel-drive from Maggie Summit Road. The stream flows seven miles in a northerly direction from the 7,120-foot elevation to 5,800 feet. Five miles of the creek are considered fishable.

Rainbow trout are the dominant species. The last stream survey estimated the population at 2,232 fish per mile, but they average just under 9 inches long.

For the hiking angler this is a beautiful stream lined with willow, wild rose and dotted with aspen and cottonwood trees in the lower elevations. Picture perfect fall fishing.

Blue Jacket Creek

Blue Jacket is a west slope stream. The creek first flows into Columbia Creek and then Bull Run Creek on the west side of Maggie Summit. Access is via Nevada 226 then improved dirt road through Bull Run Basin. Drive-in anglers need permission from the IL Ranch to get access by four-wheel-drive. Courtesy dictates getting permission to hike-in also.

The stream is 4.8 miles long and beaver activity has added quality pools and structure for the rainbow and brook trout. Rainbows, according to fisheries biologists, average 237 fish per mile and brookies average 92 fish per mile. Most fish are pan size, however.

Fly fishermen will find challenging angling along this small stream. Trout rise eagerly to dry flies imitating the creek mayflies, caddisflies and stoneflies. In the upper section aspen and fir add to the diverse scenery. The lower private section is dominated by sagebrush and scattered aspens.

Bull Run Creek

Bull Run Creek is another stream within the IL Ranch and Bull Run Basin. Get permission before trespassing.

Inside the confines of the basin that bears it name, Bull Run is a heavily-grazed creek. Below Maggie Summit Road, the stream changes character noticeably. The best fishing, however, is probably in the canyon below Bull Run Reservoir.

Historically, Bull Run Creek was stocked with rainbow trout, except the section below the Bull Run Reservoir. Rainbow and brook trout are the game fish and can reach over 10 inches.

Columbia Creek

Another Bull Run Basin stream, Columbia Creek access is via privately-controlled road. From there it is either walk-in or take a horse. The lower four miles of Columbia is private property and the upper four miles is U.S. Forest Service land.

Look for active and abandoned beaver dams. They mean good pool structure for trout and often the bigger fish live here. Above the Forest Service boundary, brush, aspen and fir feed the beaver and shade the water.

During 1987, brook trout averaged 464 fish per miles and rainbow trout average 116 fish per mile. All fish sampled that year were small, but it is difficult to capture big trout living behind beaver dams.

Foreman Creek

An east-flowing stream, Foreman Creek runs into the North Fork of the Humboldt River south of Wild Horse Reservoir. Most of the fishable and accessible water lies within the Humboldt National Forest boundaries.

Just over eight miles of stream flows through Forest Service land. A narrow, shallow stream to be sure, but home to native cutthroat trout. One of too few remaining streams holding native trout.

Even with four-wheel-drive access or high clearance two-wheel-drive, if the road is dry, expect to walk a few miles to reach the water. Turn west from Nevada Highway 225 toward the Evans Ranch.

Gance Creek

Gance Creek is an east slope stream in the Independance Mountains. The creek crosses Nevada Highway 225 five miles north of its intersection with Highway 226. An improved dirt road two miles beyond the creek crossing leads to the creek within the Humboldt National Forest.

This is another native cutthroat trout stream. The most recent stream survey estimates the cutthroat population at 145 fish per mile. Cutthroat are abundant in this small creek, but most are small. During the mid 1950s, beaver dams made quality holding water for Nevada's state fish. By the late 1970s the beaver and their dams were gone. Above the Forest Service boundary, willows dominate the riparian vegetation. The lower stretches, however, have the better fishing in normal water years.

Jack Creek

This is a drive-to stream with a campground on the west slope of the Independence Mountains. Take Nevada Highway 226—34 miles from the intersection of Highway 225—and an improved dirt road to reach the stream. A U.S. Forest Service campground 1 1/5 miles from the highway has eight campsites. Along the highway is Jack's Creek Lodge.

Approximately 4 1/2 miles of stream is fishable. Because of its easy access, the stream is heavily fished. Still, the latest stream survey records estimate as many as 2,125 rainbow trout and 316 brook trout per mile.

Willow, alder and aspen form main stream cover. In the upper reaches there are only willows.

North Fork Humboldt River

Like Gance Creek, the North Fork crosses Nevada Highway 225 about 46 miles north of Elko. A good gravel road leads west another five miles to the Humboldt Forest boundary.

The river's total length is nearly 100 miles, but only six miles around the U.S. Forest Service campground is considered fishable. Above the campground are beaver dams that could potentially shelter some large trout.

Again, native cutthroat trout are the primary sport fish. The population is estimated at 500 fish per mile up to the 7,190-foot elevation. Most of the cutthroat are small.

Brook trout also inhabit the North Fork of the Humboldt River. Brookies are more common along the lower stretch in and just outside the Forest Service boundary.

Pratt Creek

North of Elko, 43 miles via Nevada Highway 225, is the dirt road that leads to Pratt Creek. Seven miles of improved dirt road accesses the Humboldt Forest. Another five miles of true Nevada jeep trail parallels the stream. In addition to a good four-wheel-drive, fishermen need permission to access the Forest Service water.

The best fishing is above the Forest Service boundary. Here the target is a wild population of brook trout. Their numbers are small and only a few fish grow longer than 9 or 10 inches.

Pratt Creek is for hiking anglers with a desire to explore. They will even find a few primitive campsites above the Forest Service boundary.

Trail Creek

Five miles south of Mountain City, Trail Creek crosses Highway 225 near Maggie Summit Road. The stream is over 10 miles long and has an average gradient of only 2 percent.

Most of the catchable fish live about three to eight miles above the creek's confluence with the East Owyhee River. Fortunately the Maggie Summit Road parallels the stream in this same area. There is some private land involved, however.

The rainbow trout population averages around 750 fish per mile. The brook trout population is smaller at 380 fish per mile. A few of the brookies can reach the 11-inch size.

The algae and rooted aquatic vegetation are the food base for mayflies, caddisflies and stoneflies. Also Trail Creek has a good population of Paiute sculpins. Fly fishermen should bring their Muddler Minnows.

Beaver activity up to the mid-elevations means cover for fish. As always with deep still waters backed up by a beaver dam, approach is critical.

Brush shouldn't overwhelm most fly fishermen. A moderate amount of shrubbery, mostly willows, lines the banks with some aspen in the mid-elevations.

Willow Creek Reservoir

The average Nevada angler has to go out of their way to reach Willow Creek Reservoir. A 640-surface-acre swimming-pool-shaped reservoir, Willow Creek sits alongside a dirt road that roughly parallels Interstate 80. Getting there includes driving through one of the state's most active mining areas.

Eastbound fishermen traveling Interstate 80 turnoff at Golconda east of Winnemucca. There is 16 miles of blacktop here and then 40 miles of graded gravel. Westbound drivers need to turn north from Elko onto Nevada 225. Turn onto Nevada 226 as if driving to Wilson or Dry Creek reservoirs. From Taylor Canyon, before reaching the Highway Maintenance Station, a green and white sign will point west toward Tuscarora and Willow Creek. It is approximately 29 miles over good gravel road to the water.

Because this reservoir's drainage system is low-lying desert hills, the water is turbid. Clay soil stays suspended in the water.

Historically, the system of streams above the reservoir is native cutthroat trout country. The cuts still inhabit the streams and occasionally work their way down to the reservoir. Lahontan cutthroat are a hardy fish. Considering that water temperatures fluctuate up to 30 degrees a day during spawning season, it is not surprising other trout don't do well at Willow Creek.

Recent management emphasis at Willow Creek Reservoir centers on warm-water fish. White crappie, largemouth bass, channel catfish and white catfish now live in the lake. During 1994 creel checks, biologists recorded crappies averaging almost 10-inches long and bass averaging 14 inches. The largest crappie, however, was taken in 1986 and weighed over a pound.

Primitive camping is available between the road and the reservoir. Don't expect shade or even a picnic table, however. Finding level ground is as good as it gets. Still, some supplies are available in Midas roughly 16 miles west of the reservoir.

Jarbidge Mountains

When locals talk about the Jarbidge, they mean the whole range. Visitors however, usually refer to the "Wilderness Area". The Jarbidge Range has five peaks over 10,000 feet tall. Still the range does not have the ragged granite spine of the Ruby Mountains to the south. From these mountains spring rivers and streams of clear, cold trout-bearing water. Anglers visiting the Jarbidge find high-quality stream fishing in one of the least used wilderness areas in the nation.

Travel within the wilderness is on foot or horseback. Outside the boundary, the northern and western streams are most accessible by vehicle. Of course, the higher the elevation, the more anglers need four-wheel-drive vehicles with high ground clearance. An all-weather road from Rogerson, Idaho provides the primary access for the residents of Jarbidge. Two fair weather dirt and gravel roads run north and east from Nevada 225 south of Mountain City. On the Charleston road, drivers encounter steep grades and trailers are not advised. The Gold Creek road also has a couple of steep climbs where long or heavy recreational vehicles will have a tough time.

All of the Jarbidge streams listed below hold trout. The rivers are not wide, but do require wading to fish effectively. Smaller creeks require stalking and casting skills. All offer a unique angling adventure.

Bruneau River

Two of the three improved dirt roads leading the Bruneau River turn east from Nevada Highway 225 near Wild Horse Reservoir. The Gold Creek turn, in fact, is directly opposite the entrance to Wild Horse State Park. It is a 24-mile drive from the turn-off to the lower river. Likely the most used route, the Gold Creek road is an all-weather road. Well, it is almost an all-weather road. During winter months, only a few local ranchers living near Highway 225 can get through.

Another turn is roughly 10 miles south of the Gold Creek turn. This route leads to the abandoned site of Charleston and skirts the western edge of the Jarbidge Wilderness. Eventually the Charleston road reaches the town of Jarbidge. The final access is from Rogerson, Idaho and through the Jarbidge River canyon where anglers connect with one of the above roads.

Twenty-two miles of the Bruneau, the middle section, runs through the Humboldt National Forest. Another five miles of lower river flows through private land. The middle section is paralleled by a privately controlled access road. Here, the canyon is not extremely steep, but the road is narrow and can present a problem for long recreational vehicles. Both the Gold Creek and Charleston Roads connect with the Bruneau River Road.

While areas of river bank are covered with thick stands of brush-like willow and alder, the stream itself is between 12 1/2 and 28 feet wide. Get past the brush and access is good except during spring run-off.

Insect life is abundant for fly fishermen. Mayflies and caddisflies dominate, but stoneflies are a rare find. Since the Bruneau is not a steep gradient stream and lacks oxygenating riffles, stoneflies don't do well here. Snails do live in the aquatic vegetation and so do dragonflies, damselflies and crayfish.

Redband rainbow trout were last estimated at 112 fish per mile and the whitefish population was 16 fish per mile. The average size trout is in the 9- to 10-inch range. The number of trout and whitefish is likely controlled by such things as quality cover and deep pools.

Camping is allowed near the Gold Creek and Charleston roads. It is primitive, however and camp fires are discouraged. Along the middle section road it is also possible to camp, but in most places you'll think you're sleeping in the middle of the road.

Copper Creek

Just west of the Jarbidge Wilderness and downhill from the Charleston Road is Copper Creek Basin. Access is limited to a couple of four-wheel-drive roads from the Charleston Road near Coon Creek Summit. This is the stream's headwaters. Down stream access is guaranteed by an agreement between Nevada's Division of Wildlife and the Prunty Ranch. Copper Creek flows into the Bruneau River.

The upper seven miles of stream is within the Humboldt National Forest. The lowest one-mile section flows through Bureau of Land Management controlled land. In between is a half-mile section of private stream.

Active beaver colonies make for interesting and challenging fishing. Small-stream anglers know the biggest and smartest trout live in the deep water behind beaver dams.

Copper Creek redband rainbow have a good food source. Mayflies and caddisflies are common and stoneflies are also present. Also a few rough fish live in the stream.

Camping is available, but it is primitive. When accessing the stream by four-wheel-drive, anglers staying overnight will want to build camp fires. Caution is advised, however, as a wild fire in this country would be devastating.

West Fork Jarbidge River

Of the two north-flowing forks of the Jarbidge River, the West Fork is the most accessible. A graded dirt road parallels the river at the bottom of a deep canyon. Close to the Idaho border, the forks of the Jarbidge cut through spectacular vertical rock walls.

Do not bring motorhomes or large trailers into this canyon. The road is windy, often one lane wide and the climb out of the canyon is extremely steep. In fact, recreational vehicle drivers will see a sign on the Charleston Road access warning, "Narrow Road Ahead—Steep Grade In Excess of 15%—Not suitable for camper or motorhome traffic."

Anglers willing to make the trip, however, can visit Nevada's most remote town. Jarbidge was originally a mining community. Today it is a stop for big game hunters, wilderness hikers and fishermen. The river runs cool and clear except during spring run-off. During 1995, the town was isolated from the rest of the world by deep snow drifts and then by flooding. The locals don't seem to mind.

Nevada stocks the West Fork with rainbow trout. Around town these fish fall prey to the town's young fishermen using lures and bait. Above and below, however, some fish winter-over and they can reach 12 inches or longer. The last population survey estimated the West Fork held 978 rainbow trout per mile.

Rainbow trout live among the rocks and tangled roots on the West Fork of the Jarbridge River.

Closer to the West Fork's headwaters anglers can find Dolly Varden. This western char was officially re-named bull trout. In 1985, a 4-pound, 6-ounce bull was entered into the Nevada Trophy Fish program. That same year biologists estimated the population at 74 fish per mile. They inhabit the upper half of the river in Nevada.

East Fork Jarbidge River

Islands of steep, rimrock-bordered mountains separate the forks of the Jarbidge River. The East Fork is 110 miles from Elko via Rogerson, Idaho. South of the state line the river is accessible only by jeep trail at Robinson Hole. One of Nevada's most remote streams, the river is paralleled by horse and foot trails in most areas.

Of Nevada's 18-mile portion of the East Fork, 16 miles are considered fishable. Rainbow trout and bull trout (Dolly Varden) are the only game fish. A 1-pound, 5-ounce bull trout was landed in 1976. Speckled dace and sculpins also live in the river.

Insect life is abundant in the cold, clear waters of the East Fork. Caddisflies, blackflies and mayflies are abundant. Also look for stoneflies, midges and a few leeches.

The East Fork of the Jarbidge River is an excellent fly fishing stream. Its remote location guarantees light pressure.

Lime Creek

East of the Jarbidge River system is a small stream for anglers who like to explore. Lime Creek is accessible via the Pole Creek Road from the O'Neil Basin and from Idaho between Rogerson and Murphy Hot Springs. The Pole Creek road is a good road, but bring a good four-wheel-drive to reach Lime Creek. Another access is from the O'Neil Basin via four-wheel-drive roads in the Wilson Canyon area. Of course, some anglers will choose to walk.

Redband rainbow inhabit this small stream and a 1995 stream survey estimates they number 448 fish per mile. Just over three miles of fishable creek flows through the Humboldt National Forest and another mile crosses private land.

In addition to the insects fly fishermen expect to see, Lime has good numbers of forage fish in the form of speckled dace and Paiute sculpins. Take along a few streamers.

Martin Creek

Another small stream, Martin Creek is east of Wild Horse Reservoir and Nevada Highway 225. Take the Gold Creek Road from Wild Horse State Recreation Area for five miles to reach the lower end of the stream. From the Humboldt Forest boundary, a low-standard road parallels the stream another four miles. Ten miles of Martin Creek flows through public land. Only the lower 1.6 miles cross private property. Improved campsites are nearby along the Gold Springs Road.

Rainbow and brook trout live in this small stream. Despite abundant numbers of mayflies, caddisflies and midges, an eight-inch trout is a big fish.

While most Nevada anglers won't head out to fish just Martin Creek, it is a good small stream. The fact that an improved campground and improved dirt road bring anglers close to its banks makes it worth fishing.

McDonald Creek

A tributary of the Bruneau River, McDonald Creek is over 12 miles long and mostly on public land. Only 1 1/2 miles of stream, however, is open to vehicle traffic. A four-wheel-drive road connects lower McDonald with the Bruneau. Another jeep trail crosses the upper stream. The lower four miles of the creek flow through a narrow and steep sloped canyon

Yes, few Nevada anglers will make the trip to McDonald Creek. Those who treasure remote fishing in a rugged setting, however, will enjoy the drive as much as the fishing. Camping near McDonald is allowed, but, like getting there, conditions are primitive.

Redband rainbow inhabit this small mountain stream. A 1990 survey put the population at 415 trout per mile and the biggest fish measured eight inches. Mayflies and caddisflies provide an abundant food source for the trout. Also, there are a few stoneflies in the stream.

Meadow Creek

Meadow Creek runs alongside the Gold Creek Road from its confluence with the Bruneau River most the way to Big Bend Campground. This small stream is 11 1/2 miles long, but only two miles of it flow through private land.

Meadow Creek had active beaver colonies at one time. Because of the beaver and the relatively low land gradient, the fishing is mainly in pools. Rainbow trout, up to 435 fish per mile, take advantage of the cool calm water behind old beaver dams or close to exposed roots.

As the stream name implies, Meadow Creek flows through a meadow. This means anglers can expect to cast around tall sagebrush, willows and dogwood. At times the streamside vegetation is very thick. Also, depending on water conditions, areas of the creek's banks can be marsh-like.

This creek has a good variety of insects. Caddisflies and mayflies are the most abundant food source, but the stream also has stoneflies, snails, scuds and dragonflies.

Merritt Creek

One mile south of Mountain City turn east from Nevada Highway 225. Eleven miles of rough road will take you over Yankee Bill Summit and down the other side to Sagehen Basin. This basin forms the drainage for Merritt Creek.

The fishable length of Merritt is paralleled by a two-wheel drive-dirt road. However, about two-thirds of the stream below Walker Creek is private land. According to stream survey reports, the stream averages 6 1/2 feet wide and 6 inches deep, with over eight miles of fishable stream.

Abandoned and active beaver dams back up the water to form good trout water. Both brook and rainbow trout grow fat behind the dams. Before the latest prolonged drought, fisheries biologists estimated there were 1,338 rainbows per mile and another 1,056 brookies per mile.

The trout are numerous in Merritt Creek and access is good. Most of the trout, however, are found above Sagehen Basin where hiking is the best mode of transportation.

Boies Reservoir

This is a reservoir few people set out to fish. Rather, they stop on their way to or from Twin Falls, Idaho on U.S. 93, or while out hunting. Boies Reservoir sits in a remote corner of Nevada located 44 miles north of Wells and 33 miles south of Jackpot.

Boies has 62 surface acres and is 16 feet deep when full. Only 30 percent of the capacity is publicly owned, however. Land around the reservoir is private property, but fishing and camping access is allowed. Camping is primitive as there are no facilities at the lake.

Access is via U.S. Highway 93 where a green sign with white lettering marks the turn to the west. Six miles of good two-wheel-drive gravel road leads to the reservoir. Expect to share the road and the reservoir with the landowner's cattle. They won't mind if you don't.

Trout growth rates at Boies is comparable to other Elko County big trout waters like Ruby Marsh and Crittenden Reservoir. Fish stocked during spring measure 9 to 10 inches long. By fall, when the hunters arrive, the same fish can reach 15 inches or more.

Abundant aquatic weeds and invertebrates fuel the trout's food chain. Fly fishermen should expect to find good populations of scuds, water boatmen, mosquitoes, midge, snails, damselflies, dragonflies and mayflies. The fact the reservoir was drawn down in 1994 should help the aquatic wildlife bloom at Boies Reservoir.

An extra attraction for anglers fishing Boies is largemouth bass. The shallow reservoir, thick weeds and abundant feed lets the bass reach the 16- to 18-inch range. Good growth for a reservoir that freezes over every winter.

Car-top boats and float tubes are a perfect match for Boise. Boats with motors may have trouble getting through the aquatic weeds as the reservoirs drops late in the irrigation season.

O'Neil Basin

This remote corner of the Sagebrush Sea is included for the wandering angler. Those who have the desire to see new water and explore new ground.

All but two of the streams in this area flow through a natural drainage basin called the O'Neil Basin. With one exception, these streams originate in the Jarbidge Mountains and the Humboldt National Forest.

The O'Neil Basin is situated north of Interstate 80 near the Idaho border and southwest of Jackpot, Nevada. Two major access points involve driving over several miles of good, graded dirt and gravel roads. From Interstate 80 turnoff at Wells. Gas up at the quick stop gas stations and drive through old downtown. Cross the railroad tracks and follow the signs pointing to Metropolis. Metropolis

O'Neil Basin ranching has a long history in this remote corner of Nevada.

is a ghost town, but the road comes close to the old town site before working its way north and west. Stay on the blacktop and do not turn south back toward the interstate. After leaving the asphalt road stay on the wide, graded road and follow the Bureau of Land Management signs.

Also from Interstate 80, turnoff at Deeth which is between Elko and Wells. Go south, but turn left onto the dirt road before crossing the railroad tracks. This route leads under the freeway and then north through the Mary's River Basin.

Another route turns west from U.S. Highway 93 roughly 39 miles north of Wells and 27 miles south of Jackpot. This road goes past Boies Reservoir and crosses the Cold Springs Mountains.

Ranching dominates O'Neil Basin. In the lower elevations most of the basin is private land. To reach public waters, anglers will need a four-wheel-drive vehicle, be willing to walk, or willing to hire an outfitter.

Camp Creek

An eastern drainage stream, Camp Creek originates inside the Jarbidge Wilderness. Below the North Fork of Camp Creek, the main branch is 15 feet wide and averages four inches deep. Above the North Fork, the stream flows through a narrow, rocky canyon.

Nearly three decades ago Camp Creek flooded and damaged the North Fork and the lower stream. Old growth trees and brush between these two areas on the creek held and the fishery survived.

At the last stream survey the rainbow trout held in the upper stream and numbered about 143 fish per mile. Downstream, closer to the South Fork of Salmon Falls River, brown trout numbered 53 fish per mile.

Lower Camp Creek flows through private land. Access is possible, however, on two- and four-wheel-drive roads connecting with the O'Neil Basin and Pole Creek roads.

During the summer of 1995 the sign for the Wildcat Guard station was taken down. Still, the sign posts have proven to be an accurate landmark. The Wildcat Guard Station is an access point from the O'Neil Basin side of the Jarbidge Mountains.

Canyon Creek

This stream crosses the Pole Creek Road roughly six miles east of Pole Creek Guard Station. Another fork of the stream begins to the south inside the Jarbidge Wilderness.

Canyon Creek is over 36 miles long. The stream has an average width of 11 feet and is relatively deep at an average of five inches. The stream's gradient averages 2.8 percent on the lower BLM portions.

Speaking of the BLM land, grazing is allowed so there isn't a lot of brush or tall grass. Up stream on the Forest Service land, however, active beaver colonies add to the trout cover.

Rainbow trout inhabit most of Canyon Creek. Some areas of water diverted for irrigation may not hold trout, however. Also, during dry years the fish move upstream. In 1980 the rainbow trout population was estimated at 142 fish per mile. A seven-inch fish is big in this creek.

Cottonwood Creek

Cottonwood Creek crosses the O'Neil Basin road about four miles south of the O'Neil school. All three branches of this creek originate high in the Jarbidge Wilderness.

Two-wheel-drive and four-wheel-drive roads follow the creek to within one mile of the Humboldt Forest boundary. From there anglers must walk or ride-in on horseback. This system of winding roads actually connects with the Pole Creek Road near Cottonwood. Going south, the roads cross Camp Creek and T Creek.

Rainbow are the sportfish living in Cottonwood Creek. Some fish reach the 11-inch-plus size and most of the estimated 923 trout per mile are considered catchable size.

Fly fishermen will find mostly open areas, free of tall plants, near the stream. Insect life includes mayflies, caddisflies, Diptera (midges and blackflies) and dragonflies. Bring a few streamer patterns too because the creek also has rough fish like suckers and dace.

Marys River

The Marys River does not actually flow into the O'Neil Basin. It is included here because the river is accessed along the O'Neil Basin Road. North of Interstate 80 from Deeth or Wells, the road parallels the river until the sign that signals a hard right turn to the O'Neil Basin. Don't turn, keep going straight and follow the main road, unmarked at last visit, until you cross the river on a one-lane steel bridge.

On the southeast side of Marys River Peak, elevation 10,570 feet, the river begins in a permanent spring. Roughly eight miles downhill the river exits the Jarbidge Wilderness. The next three miles of the river remain inside the Humboldt Forest. From the forest to the clearly marked private land, the river flows through BLM controlled land.

Outside the wilderness, the river courses through occasionally steep canyons and wide meadows. When water flows permit, cutthroat trout hide in deep holes and around root-snags. Occasionally the cutts reach the 18-inch range.

Lahontan cutthroat have brought a lot of attention to the Marys River. This hardy native trout is on the threatened species list and the Marys River has some of them. Bureau of Land Management land swaps and exclosure fencing projects have begun to rehabilitate streamside habitat. As the current prolonged drought ends, fish still living in the upper drainage will again inhabit most of the river.

Wild Lahontan cutthroat adapt quickly to their high-desert environment. When winter snow and rain causes the river to swell, adult cutts begin moving upstream. After spawning during spring, the adults move downriver again to summer over in the deep pools of the lower river. Young-of-the-year trout swim downstream as the adults begin moving upriver the next winter.

Marys River holds the promise of harboring large wild trout again. Even during August, when flows are low, the river has abundant populations of mayflies and caddisflies. Stoneflies also live in the riffles.

Salmon Falls River

Also known as Salmon Falls Creek, this stream flows north from Sun Creek to the O'Neil Ranch and School. From here it turns east through a steep canyon only to emerge alongside U.S. Highway 93 where the river turns north again and crosses the Idaho border near Jackpot.

Winter means low-water conditions. Anglers must stalk fish this time of year.

Inside the O'Neil Basin access is limited because of private property. The Boies Ranch, located just west of U.S. 93, has let anglers access the steep canyon between the highway and the Basin. Private landowners also control some stream access north of the Boies Ranch. There are, however, places where fishermen can reach the water.

At times, again as a product of water flows, Salmon Falls has produced 20-inch brown trout and rainbows over 10 inches. All of the ingredients are here, including a good source of food in the form of insects and forage fish.

Streamside vegetation is primarily sagebrush and occasional willows or dogwood. Fly fishermen will find the vegetation to be only a slight hindrance.

North Fork Salmon Falls River

Few willows or other tall plants hinder fly fishermen on the North Fork. The difficulty, however, is getting access from private landowners. Fortunately the upper river crosses several miles of BLM land. Ten miles of the river's fishable 91 miles is open to the public.

Getting at the public land involves driving to the north end of the O'Neil Basin Road. Past the last ranch low-standard dirt roads cross the stream twice and roughly parallel it. Nevada Division of Wildlife biologists say the drive is over seven miles of low-standard roads and nine miles of remote roads.

The higher the angler goes the more rainbow trout they will find. One survey put the rainbow population at 378 fish per mile and several reached the 10-inch range. As with other area streams, brown trout like the lower elevations. Smaller in number, roughly 40 per mile, browns tend to grow larger—11 inches and more.

Sun Creek

An upper Salmon Falls River tributary, Sun Creek flows easterly from the Jarbidge Mountains. Access is from Interstate 80 about 51 miles north of Deeth in the O'Neil Basin Road. From the main road, an unimproved dirt two-wheel-drive road exists along the stream. This becomes a four-wheel-drive road during wet weather.

Spring run-off had widened and flattened the stream channel at the time of the last stream survey. Also, beaver activity was reducing the amount of tall plants shading the stream. Still, biologists estimate the Sun Creek's trout population at 776 rainbows per mile mixed with a few brook trout. While brookies can reach six inches, the rainbows reached 10-inches-plus. Ten miles of creek is considered fishable.

T Creek

Like Marys River, T Creek holds wild Lahontan cutthroat trout. Also like the Marys River to the west, the fish have suffered under a prolonged drought.

T Creek actually parallels the Marys River, but it's about three to five miles to the east. From Deeth take the O'Neil Basin Road 33 miles and turn as if going to Marys River. Instead of driving west, however, turn east to cross T Creek.

The Division of Wildlife lists three miles of T Creek's 11-mile length as fishable. Over 62 percent of the creek flows through Forest Service land. The private land is close to the creek's confluence with Marys River.

Insect life in T Creek also parallels that in Marys River. Also subject to grazing, T Creek in many ways is typical of this areas small streams.

Tabor Creek

Actually, Tabor Creek flows into the Marys River which courses south to the Humboldt River. Like the Marys, this stream is included here because it crosses the O'Neil Basin Road roughly 25 miles north of Interstate 80 at Deeth.

From O'Neil Road, an unimproved two-wheel-drive road parallels the stream for about four miles. Another three-miles-plus of fishable water is accessed on foot.

Since this is a popular stream with local anglers, the Bureau of Land Management has put in a few picnic tables for campers. Anglers fishing Tabor will see them just upstream of the cattle guard marking the BLM boundary.

Roughly 88 percent of Tabor's rainbow are wild trout although the stream is stocked regularly. The fish can reach 10 inches or more, but the average is closer to seven inches.

Fly fishermen will like the abundant mayflies, caddisflies, stoneflies and midges. Most fly casters, however, will not appreciate the thick stands of willow and dogwood. Those who like the challenge of fly fishing small streams will quickly fall in love with this easily-reached desert stream.

Crittenden Reservoir

Special regulations and its remote location make Crittenden Reservoir one of the major trophy trout fisheries in the state. At 260 surface acres, the reservoir is the right size for float tubes and car-top boats.

Rainbow trout grow to 11 pounds in the rich aquatic waters of Crittenden. While trout that large are not common, 18-inch versions are frequently landed. Largemouth bass also live in the reservoir. During warm-water conditions, when the trout hold deep, small bass seem to outnumber the trout. The largest Crittenden bass entered in the Trophy Fish Program weighed 5 pounds 8 ounces.

Most of the lake is a shallow littoral zone that harbors phenomenal populations of *Callibaetis* mayflies and midges. Caddisflies, damselflies and dragonflies

Bass make an interesting diversion for trout fishermen visiting Crittenden Reservoir.

round out the trout's diet. Combined with good cover for stocked trout, Crittenden Reservoir trout show impressive growth rates.

Crittenden is located on private land 17 miles northwest of Montello, Nevada. To reach the reservoir, turn north from Interstate 80 at exit 378. The road is Nevada Highway 233 and lies 59 miles east of Wells. Montello is a railroad and ranching community 23 miles from the freeway. Some supplies, meals and gas are available here. I personally have not stopped at the Cow Shed Bar, but it looks colorful.

At the north end of town, turn west. Look for a small brown BLM sign. The improved gravel road to the lake allows 35 miles per hour or more in some places. The last turn is about 160 degrees to the right, so slow down when going past 12 Mile Ranch.

Camping at the reservoir is prohibited. Look for primitive campsites uphill from the reservoir and a few spots below the earthen dam.

Angel Lake

Seemingly carved out of a solid rock cliff, Angel Lake is actually a depression in the granite. In 1880, a dam was added to allow downstream irrigation. Located at 8,000 feet above sea level, this 13-surface-acre snow melt and spring-fed lake offers drive-up alpine angling. The 35-foot-deep lake is drawn down to 25 feet deep and about 11 surface acres by the end of every irrigation season.

What makes this rainbow and brook trout lake inviting is the scenery and the access. The lake and its 26-site campground, looks east over a broad expanse of desert. An extremely steep climb via paved road, however, can strain the engine of large recreational vehicles. Another 16-site campground is located at the base of the steep grade. From May through October, the campgrounds fill virtually every weekend. Plan ahead and call 800/280-2367 for reservations.

The road from Interstate 80 at Wells is well marked, except maybe the turns around Chimney Rock Municipal Golf Course. Look for a brown and white sign at exit 351 on the interstate.

Angel Lake is a put-and-take fishery—rainbows, brookies and a few tiger trout. A few surprises linger beneath the lake's surface. In 1993 a 20 1/4-inch, 3-pound 12-ounce tiger trout was entered in the Nevada Trophy Fish Program.

All forms of tackle catch Angel Lake trout. The record book doesn't tell us what tactic caught the big tiger trout, however. This is a float tube lake, if you want to use a watercraft. Car-top and trailered boats won't find a place to launch.

High-country lakes tend to be on the small side, but they're big on scenery.

Ruby Mountain High Lakes

Driving from Elko to Wells on Interstate 80 you cannot help but see the Rubies. Giant granite peaks seem to jump out of the surrounding smooth sagebrush-covered hills.

Named for what westward-bound immigrants thought were true rubies, this mountain range is an alpine wilderness in the middle of the desert. Anglers, however, will find the mountains are landlocked. Private land surrounds nearly the entire range. The best and most popular access is through Lamoille Canyon 13 miles south of Elko on Nevada Highway 227. There is some access north of Ruby Marshes and over Secret Pass (Nevada 229) also.

The main method of transportation is either on foot or by horseback. Yes, this is remote and rugged country. Just the kind of solitude that appeals to those who like to explore.

Most of the waters that follow have only primitive camping available. Pack it in and pack it out is the rule. Lamoille Canyon, however, does have two public campgrounds that offer some amenities for a reasonable fee.

Cold Lakes

Northeast of Lamoille between Green Mountain (10,828-foot elevation) and Old Man of the Mountain, Cold Lakes sit at 9,000 feet. Springs and snow melt feed this high-country lake. Cold Lakes are two adjacent lakes. The upper lake is 3.7 surface acres and has a maximum depth of 28 feet. Smaller at 1.8 surface acres, the lower lake is 24 feet deep. Outflow forms the Middle Fork of Cold Creek.

Access is best via a 4 1/2-mile trail up the Middle Fork of Cold Creek. However, this route crosses private property at the trailhead. Get permission before trespassing. At one time the U.S. Forest Service was trying to acquire public access, but they were still negotiating at last report.

Originally stocked with brook and rainbow trout, an eradication project in 1960 led the way for golden trout stocking. The goldens failed to survive. Today this is a brook-trout fishery. These lakes are managed as a wild-trout fishery.

Echo Lake

To get to Echo Lake take the Jiggs Highway (Nevada 228) from Elko and Spring Creek. Turn east through South Fork Indian Reservation approximately seven miles south of the turn for South Fork Reservoir. After passing through the reservation the lake is a six-mile hike farther up Echo Canyon. The tribe charges an access fee nearly as steep as the towering mountains.

Anglers normally fish Echo Lake by hiring a local outfitter to carry them and their gear up the mountain. The lake sits at the 9,287-foot elevation and is a tributary to the South Fork of the Humboldt River. Only 29 surface acres, Echo is 155 feet at its deepest. Over 50 percent of the lake is more than 50 feet deep. A mud and sand bottom plus the elevation limits aquatic plants and invertebrate life. There are, however, midges and water boatmen available for trout to feed on.

Brook trout are the only confirmed trout population at last report. Still anglers claim to catch a few lake trout (mackinaw) planted in 1980.

Favre Lake

One of the more popular and heavily-used Ruby Mountain lakes, Favre is accessed via Lamoille Canyon. From Elko go south on Nevada Highway 227. Look for the sign pointing south to the deep, steep canyon in the mountains.

Reaching the lake is a considerable hike from the main trailhead at the top of Lamoille Canyon, but it is a relatively easy walk. The lake draws high numbers of overnight users.

Favre is only 19 surface acres, but has a maximum depth of 45 feet. The lake's high productivity consistently maintains a large fish population. The only trout showing up in creel censuses is brook trout.

The lake bottom is mostly mud with some gravel, rubble and boulders along the shore. Food sources for the brookies include midges, damselflies and dragonflies.

Water entering Favre is from Castle and Liberty Lakes. Outflow forms the headwaters of Kleckner Creek and reaches to South Fork of the Humboldt River.

Griswold Lake

Griswold is accessed from Spring Creek south of Elko. An unimproved 2 1/2-mile trail at the mouth of Heenan Canyon proves a moderately steep hike over rocky terrain for the last mile. A private, locked gate blocks trail access, however, word is access is open to residents of Spring Creek.

Springs and snow melt form the 15 1/2-surface-acre Griswold Lake. The lake's maximum depth is 25 feet in rocky terrain. An old water control structure was once used to raise the lake's level, but it is inoperative today.

During the 1987 lake survey by Division of Wildlife biologists, Griswold held cutthroat trout up to 18 inches. The lake winterkills frequently, however, and the fishing can be limited.

Hidden Lakes

Despite their name, Hidden Lakes get moderate fishing pressure. Why look for these lakes? Would 20-inch cutthroat trout caught in an alpine wilderness make the seven-mile trip worth it? Horseback trips arranged through local outfitters make the trip easier on the feet, though not necessarily the backside. Three trails lead to Hidden Lakes.

The upper lake is smallest at 2.8 surface acres and a maximum depth of eight feet. The low lake is 6.1 surface acres and 32 feet deep. The bottom is mud, boulder and gravel in the lower lake. Good habitat for midges, caddisflies, scuds, snails and leeches.

Inflow for Hidden Lakes comes from springs and snow melt. Water leaving the lower lake joins Soldier Lake in forming the headwaters of Soldier Creek.

Island Lake

This is one of the most used lakes near the Lamoille Canyon trailhead. Access is over an improved trail from the parking lot. A small lake, Island is only 7.5 surface acres and 22 feet deep. A small island near the middle easily identifies the lake.

The lake supports a naturally-reproducing population of brook trout. There are always plenty of eager brookies in Island Lake.

The mud and sand bottom allows rooted aquatic vegetation to support good populations of midges, leeches, water boatmen, stoneflies and mayflies. Thick brush along the southern shore is only spotty and a temporary nuisance. A mostly rocky shoreline gives fishermen plenty of access.

Lamoille Lake

It is no surprise that Lamoille Lake sits at the top of Lamoille Canyon. This is the most heavily-fished high-mountain lake in the region except for Angel Lake. Lamoille is the first fishable lake found on the main trail from Lamoille Canyon parking lot. It is approximately a one-mile, easy hike.

A 13.6-surface-acre lake, Lamoille is only 20 feet at its deepest. The bedrock bottom with small amounts of mud limits the aquatic vegetation and the insect life. Midges appear to provide the main food source. Not surprising considering this lake is 9,740 feet above sea level.

Brook trout are the only species present in Lamoille. They are, however, a self-sustaining population except when severe winters lead to fish kills.

Liberty Lake

Another Lamoille Canyon lake, Liberty is a strenuous two-mile walk over Liberty Pass from the Lamoille Canyon trailhead. The Forest Service has built an improved trail, however.

Recent Division of Wildlife surveys and angler reports indicate that brook trout overpopulation and stunting is not a problem. Managed as a wild-trout fishery, the brookies are self sustaining.

Very little sand and gravel is present in the 108-foot deep Liberty Lake. Still, beneath its 21 surface acres there is some rooted aquatic vegetation and insect life. Because the lake's elevation is 10,039 feet, midges provide the main food source. A small Woolly Bugger or Marabou Leech, however, is readily taken by the wild brook trout.

Lost Lake

Nevada anglers can find Lost Lake east of the South Fork Indian Reservation off Highway 228. Public access is via Cottonwood Creek south of Rattlesnake Creek to the Humboldt Forest boundary. Rattlesnake Creek is supplemented by the outflow from Lost Lake. There is no defined trail to Lost Lake. Sounds remote, doesn't it? It is and for that reason angling pressure is very light. This is a wild-cutthroat-trout fishery. Periodic winterkills, however, limit Lost Lake's fishing potential.

Lost Lake is only 3 surface acres and 9 1/5 feet deep. The elevation is 9,872 feet.

Overland Lake

Moving to the east flank of the granite Titans called the Ruby Mountains we find Overland Lake. Public access is provided by a Forest Service trail leading from the county road connecting Ruby Marsh and Secret Pass. It is a 5 1/5-mile hike to the lake.

Overland is a wild-brook-trout fishery. The 9,453-foot elevation lake has a mud and boulder bottom that supports rooted aquatic plants. As a result, good populations of trout food, by alpine lake standards, are available to the trout. Midges, however, are the main food source. The lake's outflow forms Overland Creek. This creek flows eastward into the Ruby Valley.

Robinson Lake

Robinson is located between Cold Lake and Hidden Lakes. The lake gets moderately high use despite the lengthy hike from its three access points. One reason for the high use is its proximity to Cold Lake and Hidden Lakes, another reason is the use of horses by anglers and outfitters.

Fairly large by Ruby Mountain standards, Robinson Lake has 17.4 surface acres when full, but is only six feet deep. A mostly mud bottom leads to a rich environment for the abundant brook trout. Blackflies, leeches, scuds, midges and frogs are the protein source for trout. Though most brookies fall in the seven- to nine-inch range, some 11-inch fish have been recorded.

Robinson Lake is the headwaters for Robinson Creek which flows into the Ruby Valley.

Verdi Lake

Almost deeper than it is wide, Verdi Lake is six surface acres and 90 feet deep. Snow melt fills this deep rocky basin called a lake. The outflow forms the headwaters of Talbot Creek.

There are two ways to reach Verdi Lake. One is from the Lamoille Canyon trailhead over a poorly defined trail (lots of rocky ground) that is just over a mile long. The other is over privately-controlled access to Talbot Creek near the town of Lamoille. Expect a rigorous five-mile hike up Talbot Creek. Verdi sees only moderate fishing pressure because of the difficult access.

The mostly mud bottom in the deep areas supports little trout food. In the shallows there are some rooted plants and this is where midges, backswimmers and water beetles are found.

Only cutthroat trout were found in Verdi Lake during the last official survey. The report didn't record how many or what their sizes were.

Boulder Lake

Boulder Lake is technically in the East Humboldt Mountains, north of Secret Pass or Nevada Highway 229. This is a small brook-trout lake. With only six surface acres and a maximum depth of 10 1/2 feet, Boulder does see some winterkill during severe winters. The mostly mud bottom, however, is fertile for growing aquatic plants and insects. Look for midges, caddisflies and mayflies.

Boulder Lake gets moderately high use. This is surprising considering the only public access starts from the other side of the mountain at Weeks Access in Clover Valley. From Weeks, it is a rigorous three-mile hike to the lake. Access up Third Boulder Creek, the lake's outflow stream, is controlled by private land ownership.

Grey's Lake

Another East Humboldt Range lake, Grey's Lake sits above Starr Valley at an elevation of 8,600 feet. The 4.9-surface-acre reservoir is five feet at its deepest point, but over 50 percent of the lake is under five feet deep.

Midges, mayflies and caddisflies are the main trout forage at Grey's. The mud bottom and shallow depth promotes good plant and insect growth for the cutthroat trout. Trout are stocked between seven and 14 inches. The shallow lake does see occasional winter kill following severe winters.

Grey's Lake gets moderate use because access is limited to a four-mile Forest Service trail originating at Angel Lake. Starr Valley access up Grey's Creek is private and is by permission only.

Smith Lake

Smith Lake sits in the East Humboldt range at the 9,096-foot elevation just north of Angel Lake. A five-surface-acre, 14-foot deep cutthroat-trout lake, Smith sees some natural trout reproduction.

The bottom is mostly mud, but lacks great numbers of rooted aquatic vegetation. Good numbers of mayflies, caddisflies, midges and water beetles provide forage for trout.

For many years this shallow and remote lake went fishless. Nevada officials theorize this is the reason the lake only gets moderate fishing pressure now.

Access to Smith Lake is limited to foot and horseback traffic. If visiting Angel or Grey's lakes, Smith Lake makes an interesting stop.

Steele Lake

Steele Lake is the last, but not the least, of the East Humboldt Range lakes covered here. The outflow, Steele Creek, flows into Clover Valley south of Angel Lake.

A self-sustaining population of brook trout lives in the 9,500-foot elevation lake. Brookies do well in small lakes like this one—15 surface acres and a maximum depth of 41 feet.

Boulders, rubble and some gravel in the shallows make up Steele Lake's bottom. Aquatic plant life is limited, but trout food in the form of bloodworms, midges and water beetles is available.

Walk-in traffic is light at Steele Lake. Outfitters, however, stop regularly at this lake.

Ruby Mountain Streams

Small streams present a unique angling challenge. Often fishermen draw on the skills and tactics learned over several seasons to catch trout in clear alpine streams. Other times, greedy trout rush to the fly or lure in under-fished remote creeks. Streams in the Ruby Mountains fit into both categories.

As described in the section on Ruby Mountain High Lakes, access to these streams is limited. Much of the mountain range is ringed with private land. If, however, you like to explore and are willing to spend a few days among Nevada's most spectacular mountains check out the following streams.

Ackler Creek

Actually a west slope of the East Humboldt range stream, access to Ackler is through private land controlled by locked gates. A jeep trail reaches the 9,600-foot elevation close to the stream and a packer's trail crosses the basin. Most trails, however, are game and livestock trails.

Ackler is 9 1/2 miles long with only 3.2 miles within the Humboldt National Forest. The remainder is private. This a good perennial stream that averages 13 1/2 feet wide and nearly seven inches deep.

Historically, Ackler is cutthroat water, but they disappeared during the 1950s. Since then a wild brook trout fishery has taken hold. During the 1983 stream survey the population was estimated at 1,584 trout per mile at the Forest boundary and 370 per mile at the 8,100-foot elevation. That survey team reported an average size of 5.8 inches for the brookies, but they also measured some nine-inch fish.

Fly fishermen can expect to find abundant numbers of mayflies, while stoneflies and caddisflies are common too. Only scattered blackflies were located during 1983.

Much of the stream is open due to beaver activity. Thick stands of brush like willow and wild rose do exist, but don't choke off access.

Boulder Creek

Within the Humboldt National Forest, Boulder Creek has two forks and each of these have an additional two forks. The main forks are fairly rugged and the water is swift. The East Fork originates from Boulder Lake (see Ruby Mountain Lakes) and the West Fork starts from snow melt and springs along a high ridge.

Brook trout inhabit Boulder Creek and its various branches. Due to the terrain, however, the population is estimated at only 316 fish per mile. In the deeper plunge pools, anglers can find some 10-inch trout.

As knowledgeable fly fishermen would expect, Boulder Creek has three species of caddisflies, stoneflies and mayflies. Also good numbers of blackfly larvae inhabit the stream.

Corral Creek

South of Jiggs and Harrison Pass and beyond the end of Nevada Highway 228's pavement, flows Corral Creek. Permission is required to cross the Corta Ranch, but if granted a dirt road parallels the stream for 3.6 miles. Respect the landowner's wishes. If permission is denied, it is possible to walk from the Harrison Pass Road to the public portion of the creek, but the only trails were cut by wildlife.

Five miles of Corral Creek's 16-mile length is considered fishable. Approximately 54 percent of the stream is on public land. The water averages 6 1/2 feet wide, but only five inches deep.

Brook trout live in this west slope small stream. They feed on caddis, mayflies, midges and snails. Behind the stream's numerous beaver dams they likely dine on rough fish or minnows.

Green Mountain Creek

Green Mountain Creek flows from the Ruby Mountains north of Harrison Pass. After leaving Elko via Nevada 228 stay on the Harrison Pass Road (one way to the Ruby Marshes). The creek crosses the road in the lower portion of the canyon.

Access to the North Fork is by four-wheel-drive over rocky roads. Two-wheel-drive vehicles can reach the southern fork before the road becomes rough.

Seven miles of the 16-mile long Green Mountain Creek is fishable. A little narrow with an average width of seven feet, Green Mountain averages a respectable 7 3/4 inches deep. This is relatively steep country, however.

The North Fork has brook trout up to 10 inches long for roughly four miles. Above the brookies anglers will find cutthroat trout reaching nine inches for another four miles.

On the South Fork the only game fish is brook trout. Here, the brookies are a little smaller and only three miles of stream has reasonable trout habitat.

Beaver dams and feeding has led to siltation problems on Green Mountain Creek, for this reason stoneflies appear only occasionally. However, mayflies are common and caddisflies are abundant. Other insects of concern to fly fishermen include midges and water boatmen.

Like most of the streams described here, Green Mountain Creek lies within the boundaries of the Humboldt National Forest. Please obey the rules for camping and campfires when visiting these waters.

Lamoille Creek

Lamoille Creek has over 10 miles of fishable water in the canyon below Lamoille Lake. This is a popular fishery because eight miles of paved road parallels most of the stream within the Humboldt Forest. Also, the Forest Service has built two campgrounds in the canyon.

The creek's source is Lamoille Lake (see Ruby Mountain High Lakes). Cold water runs over a granite bottom mostly lined with low lying brush and bordered by large wet meadows. Look for the deepest pools in the lower three to four miles of the stream. Here, willows line the stream and the canyon walls are closer to the creek.

Brook trout grow to 10 inches and average 591 fish per mile in the upper reaches of the stream. Rainbows begin appearing at lower elevations and can reach 11 inches, but they only average 70 fish per mile. Lamoille Creek is stocked every year.

During June 1995, an exceptionally heavy snowpack and the resulting spring run off lead to flooding and mud slides. As a result Thomas Canyon Campground's 16 sites received substantial damage. By the time you read this the campground should be back in full operation. For reservations call 1-800-280-CAMP

Long Canyon Creek

Few anglers will make the effort to reach Long Canyon Creek. The South Fork Indian Tribe charges steep fees to access Long Canyon Creek. A jeep trail follows the stream for about five miles from the Forest Service boundary, but anglers must get permission to cross first.

To reach the Gund Ranch, go south from Elko on Nevada 227 and turn right onto Nevada 228. Turn east to the South Fork Indian Reservation and the small town of Lee. Continue south then east on farming roads to the ranch.

Fishermen that get permission to cross can catch three different trout. During the 1980 stream survey, brook trout inhabited three miles of stream, rainbows another two miles and cutthroat trout almost five miles.

Angler use, however, is low due to the private property and the steep mountains. The average stream gradient is high at 8 1/4 percent.

Pearl Creek

South of Corral Creek and Harrison Pass on Nevada Highway 228 is Pearl Creek. Another small stream in relatively steep terrain, Pearl has a good population of small trout. To reach Pearl Creek continue south of Corral Creek. Just over two miles of rough road parallels the creek and trails go upstream another two miles. Only 4 1/2 miles of stream are listed as fishable.

Brook trout populations up to 1,056 fish per mile were sampled in 1980. During 1984, brook trout were eradicated and cutthroat were reintroduced. A small brookie population still exists. Sampling and calculations put cutthroat trout numbers at 800 per mile. Most fish are small because the stream is small. The average width is only 11 1/2 feet and it averages four inches deep. The gradient averages a steep seven percent.

Heavy cattle use keeps streamside vegetation mowed down. Some willows next to the bank provide limited cover in the form of undercut banks.

While good numbers of mayfly nymphs and rock and stick cased caddis live in Pearl Creek, no stoneflies were found during the last stream survey.

Talbot Creek

Access to Talbot Creek is limited to a trail through private land. The creek exits the Ruby Mountains east of the town of Lamoille and Lamoille Canyon.

Over five miles of stream within the Humboldt Forest are fishable. Here, the creek has good pools, and, at lower elevations, heavy streamside cover from willows and dogwood. On average Talbot is deeper than many Ruby Mountain streams at over eight inches. Talbot is steep with an average 8 1/2 percent gradient. Still the stream averages 10 1/2 feet wide.

Brook trout are the only game fish in Talbot Creek. In 1983 biologists estimated their population at 924 fish per mile. Other stream samples found abundant mayfly nymphs, but only scattered numbers of stoneflies and caddisflies.

Among Elko area anglers Talbot Creek is a preferred, but lightly used stream.

Thorpe Creek

Keep going east from Lamoille Canyon and Talbot Creek to reach Thorpe Creek. Again limited to foot and pack trail access, private property and locked gates discourage casual anglers.

While fishing pressure at Thorpe is obviously light, reports reaching Elko say there are a good number of wild brook trout available. Brookies don't grow large in steep streams like Thorpe, so a 10-inch fish is considered a trophy. At just under 500 brook trout per mile, biologist say the average size fish is seven inches.

Like Talbot Creek, mayflies are abundant in Thorpe. Stoneflies, on the other hand, are present, but not common. Caddisflies are common.

Ruby Marsh

Also know as Ruby Lake, Ruby Marsh is the centerpiece of a 38,000-acre wildlife refuge. The Ruby Lake National Wildlife Refuge is 60 miles south of Elko and 100 miles northwest of Ely. A wetland or swamp managed primarily for water fowl, the Marsh is a network of ditches and dikes used to manage the water.

When the weather and the Ruby Mountain snowpack permits, Harrison Pass is the most popular access route. Take Nevada Highway 227 from downtown Elko—you can't miss either of the two well-marked turns. At Spring Creek turn right on Highway 228 and continue south past South Fork State Park and the town of Jiggs. As the pavement ends, an improved dirt road leads up a canyon to Harrison Pass. The Marsh is just over the mountain and to the south.

Ruby Marsh has two improved boat ramps, but they and the South Lake are closed until mid-June.

Another route is via Nevada Highway 229. This paved road crosses Secret Pass some 20 miles east of Elko near the Hallock turn off. Highway 229 also intersects U.S. 93 approximately 20 miles south of Wells. From Nevada 229 there are another 15 miles over improved dirt road to reach the marsh.

From the south take U.S. Highway 50 and turn north on a combination graded gravel and paved road about 31 miles West of Ely. It is another 50 miles to the refuge.

The Ruby Marsh is 1,000 surface acres of shallow freshwater and 7,230 acres of deep freshwater. Maximum water depth is 12 feet. Dense islands of bullrush combined with bladderwort and pondweed provide excellent cover for trout and bass. When you drive up to the lake for the first time and see how thick the bullrush is, you'll ask, "Where's the lake?"

Water for the marsh is collected from natural springs along the western edge of the refuge. This collection ditch is famous for producing big trout. We're talking rainbows, tiger trout and brown trout over 10 pounds. Nevada's record tiger trout (brook-brown hybrid) weighed 20 pounds, 13 ounces and came from the marsh. (Nevada discontinued its tiger trout program in 1996). The marsh is also in the record book for a 25-pound brown trout, a 10-pound, 8-ounce rainbow trout, 4-pound, 14-ounce brook trout and a 9-pound largemouth bass.

The collection ditch, a network of springs, has special fishing regulations.

The system of dikes at the north end of the wildlife refuge is open to dike-only fishing. From the dikes, fishermen cast flies into the north and east sumps and five small impoundments. Deep channels alongside the dike roads hold good size trout and lots of small bass. Occasionally the bass are measured by the pound and not inches.

Holdover trout, there is no natural reproduction at the marsh, love snails. Midges, dragonflies, damselflies, caddisflies and mayflies also live within the marsh's waters. Don't look for forage fish, though, there aren't any.

South of Brown Dike, the dividing line for the south lake, boats and float tubes are banned from January 1 through June 14. Only motorless boats, float tubes and boats with electric motors can access the south lake from June 15 through August 1. From August through December boats with motors up to 10 horsepower can be used. The reason for this seemingly crazy schedule is to protect nesting waterfowl.

Car-top craft can launch at any of the marsh's access areas. The south lake has two improved boat ramps. Remember this is a marsh and the water is relatively shallow.

Camping is not allowed within the refuge. The Forest Service, however, does operate a campground just outside the refuge's main gate. This campground has running water, vault toilets and trash collection. There are other campgrounds located farther away from the refuge in the Ruby Mountains. Also, some businesses in the area rent campsites. Some even come with power and water hookups. During the area's recent mining boom, however, these facilities have carried the overflow of workers seeking housing. Shanty Town is a small community south of the Forest Service campground with a small store selling gas and a few essentials.

South Fork Humboldt River

The South Fork of the Humboldt River flows 22 miles through gently sloping bench and bottom land. Most of this is private land used for cattle production. Below South Fork Reservoir's dam, the river courses another 16 miles through a canyon before entering the Humboldt River.

Despite the private land and cattle, this is the third most fished stream in northeastern Nevada. Historically, the river gets stocked with hatchery trout. The upper river, however, holds some wild rainbow and brook trout. Occasionally native cutthroat and whitefish are caught too. Also, some fish use the river above the reservoir for spawning.

Snow melt from several west-central Ruby Mountain streams combine to form the river. Below the dam, Ten Mile Creek enters the river and three miles downstream Dixie Creek enters. Extreme seasonal water fluctuations are common on the South Fork. Winter snow melt will occasionally flood the low bench land. Summer water withdrawals for irrigation can force the fish into deep pools during dry years.

The river is accessible by automobile through most of its course. Only seven miles of lower river is restricted to foot traffic. Getting to the lower river can require a four-wheel-drive. Reaching the upper river means good graded roads. The drive is over Nevada Highways 227 and 228 south of Elko for 20 miles, then eight miles south through Lee, Nevada. Another four miles of the road goes through a private ranch to the road's end. Again, access through Indian Reservation land may involve a fee.

The South Fork is a good fly fishing river. Insects living in the stream include stoneflies, mayflies, caddisflies and dragonflies. Also, there is a good population of crayfish.

At the risk of sounding optimistic, the river below South Fork Reservoir is Nevada's newest tailwater fishery. During 1995, the reservoir filled for the first time. As a result, fish washed over the spill way and local anglers had a summer full of exciting fishing. The winter of 1995-1996 promises a good snowpack that could keep this section of river on the must-fish list.

South Fork Reservoir

Nevada's newest reservoir is rapidly becoming the state's most popular fishery. No doubt the fact that South Fork lies 20 miles from the city of Elko has something to do with it.

The dam on the South Fork of the Humboldt River was completed in 1988. Water began flooding the broad river valley that summer, but the reservoir did not completely fill until early summer 1995. A prolonged drought slowed the process.

While it was filling, South Fork immediately won favor among fly fishermen as both a spring and fall trout fishery. The inlet end of the reservoir saw spring-spawning rainbows and fall-spawning brown trout.

The willows along the water eventually provided cover for minnows and habitat for insects. This means trout will cruise the area looking for food.

Since water has run over the spillway, a tailwater fishery has developed. Officials have netted some of the trout that escaped from the reservoir and moved them back to the lake. Others, however, survived the summer in the lower river.

Here the trout are measured in pounds instead of inches. At least one 9-pound South Fork rainbow trout was entered in the state's Trophy Fish Program during 1995.

Near the dam, along the rocky banks, black bass became the primary quarry. Creel checks by fisheries officials during the summer of 1995 had the average bass at 14-plus inches. Bass are a biological control for the reservoir's tui chubs. Keeping large bass in the reservoir means they can eat more chubs. Hence, Nevada has adopted special regulations for bass.

Reservoirs built in Nevada are typically very high in nutrients. It is this characteristic that makes fish grow big. And big fish make for exciting fishing. As an example, bait fishing is probably the poorest fishing technique for South Fork. A blob of bait on the bottom just doesn't work. There is so much feed in the reservoir the fish are not rummaging around on the bottom for something to eat. At first light, fish open their mouths and swallow enough food to keep going all day.

South Fork Reservoir was built strictly for recreation. For this reason, Nevada has built a state park around the now-full reservoir. Full facility campsites are located along the northern shore near a beautiful boat ramp. Steep banks limit access along the northern and southern shore. Shade, too, is a limited commodity.

Water skiing is allowed, but the inlet area has a special speed limit to protect anglers. Access near the inlet and southern shore is limited, but not impossible to find. Car-top boaters and float-tubing anglers will want to launch as close to the fishing as possible.

To get to South Forks Reservoir, leave Interstate 80 and drive into Elko. From Idaho Street, the main street, turn south towards Spring Creek and Lamoille via Nevada Highway 227. Approaching Spring Creek, Nevada 228, the Jiggs Highway, turns south. Follow it 12 miles to the northern entrance to South Fork State Park. Three miles farther is the southern entrance.

Zunino/Jiggs Reservoir

Zunino/Jiggs Reservoir is a combination private and public irrigation reservoir located approximately 30 miles south of Elko, Nevada. The reservoir, when full, has 156 surface acres with a maximum depth of 14 feet. Due to irrigation, the surface size is normally closer to 45 surface acres with a depth of 10 feet.

Historically, this reservoir can support fantastic trout growth rates. Eight-inch rainbows stocked one year can nearly double their size by the next year. In 1985, a 6-pound 15-ounce rainbow came from Zunino/Jiggs Reservoir. Also, Zunino/Jiggs is a potential bass fishery. Before the reservoir went dry in 1990, a self-sustaining population of largemouth bass coexisted with the trout. Currently this reservoir is managed as a put-grow-take rainbow fishery.

The Bureau of Land Management has built a small campground at Zunino/Jiggs Reservoir. Fishermen will find barbecue stands and picnic tables, but not much more. This campground is just above primitive.

To reach this reservoir, go south from Elko past South Fork Reservoir as if driving to Ruby Marsh over Harrison Pass. The reservoir is two miles north of the small town of Jiggs on Nevada Highway 228. Look for three entrances, all dirt roads. Each turn is marked by a large BLM sign.

CHAPTER 10: Lander County

Lander County's economy is based on mining and ranching like it was over 130 years ago. In fact, during the last century silver production around Austin, Nevada rivaled the famed Virginia City's for at least a decade.

Today Austin, a needed stop along U.S. Highway 50, is a ghost town compared to the boom of the 1860s. Battle Mountain, however, is a fast growing city along Interstate 80.

For fishermen Lander County is important for two reasons. One reason is the Toiyabe Mountains (see Nye County in Region III). Many of the streams in this mountain range go ignored by anglers. The other reason Lander County is important is two private fly fishing ranches: Iowa Canyon Trout Ranch and Smith Creek Ranch.

Accommodations, hotels and restaurants, are limited to Battle Mountain and Austin. Anglers find few stores catering to their needs in either town.

Interstate 80 and U.S. Highway 50 cross the county going east and west. North and south routes include Nevada Highway 305 between Austin and Battle Mountain and Nevada 376 from U.S. 50 near Austin to U.S. 6 near Tonopah.

Nevada's history includes boom-and-bust mining, and ranching.

Groves Lake

It is difficult to separate Groves Lake from Kingston Creek. The creek flows into and out of the lake. In fact, the reservoir is a wide spot in Kingston Canyon. For continuity, however, this book will treat the two waters separately.

Groves Lake is an excellent fishery supported by annual stocking and a self-sustaining population of brown trout. At roughly nine surface acres and a maximum depth of 15 to 20 feet, this is an ideal float-tube reservoir. The only problem is that the dam leaks. As a result, the reservoir stays close to minimum pool most of the year.

Stocking rainbow trout at Groves helps absorbs some fishing pressure. On a busy weekend, Groves is packed with anglers. The put-and-take fishery helps protect the wild brown trout. Some rainbows manage to evade the rush of summer fishermen, however. During the fall of 1995, an 11-pound-plus rainbow was taken from Groves Lake.

Camping is available below the reservoir in a Forest Service Campground. Twelve sites with barbecues, tables and two vault toilets sit along the creek below the lake. During the summer, a fee is charged.

Groves Lake is located 6 1/2 miles west of Nevada Highway 376. The turn is roughly 15 miles south of U.S. 50 and 83 miles north of U.S. 6. Look for a green and white sign announcing Kingston two miles.

Iowa Canyon Trout Ranch

Iowa Canyon is one of Lander County's two pay-to-fish fly fishing reservoirs. The reservoir is 27 surface acres on the west flank of the Toiyabe Range north of the Toiyabe National Forest. From U.S. Highway 50 turn north on Nevada 305 for 26 miles, or from Battle Mountain go south on Highway 305 roughly 60 miles. The ranch is east of the highway over four miles of graded road.

Rainbow trout weighing two to six pounds were available in 1995. By the time you read this the fish will have grown substantially. The trout in this reservoir are famous for being among the strongest in the state. Bring strong tippets and a good rod.

The reservoir is rich in aquatic life. All of the typical lake insect life hides within the weed beds close to shore. Fly anglers like float tubing this water, but wading is possible near the dam.

Back at the rustic turn-of-the-century brick ranch house, fishermen receive royal treatment. If desired, the full-service package includes a two bedroom, two bath bunkhouse with four double beds and a kitchenette. Trailer parking, campsites and restrooms and showers are available too.

For details and booking information call Jim Parish at (702) 426-8053.

Groves Lake receives regular plants of rainbow trout, but a few fish hold-over every year.

Smith Creek Ranch

Another private fly fishing reservoir, Smith Creek ranch is located between U.S. Highway 50 and Nevada Highway 722. Highway 722 crosses the Desatoya Mountains at Carroll Summit. At the bottom of the east flank of the mountains turn north for 13 miles over a graded gravel road to reach the ranch.

Smith Creek opened with a six-acre, man-made trout pond during the spring of 1995. At that time the fish ranged in size from three to 12 pounds. The average fish weighed in at a healthy five pounds. Like all private trout fisheries, this is fly fishing with single hook, barbless flies only. All fish are released.

The ranch hopes to open an 27-surface-acre reservoir during 1997. If successful, the six-acre pond will be used only to raise fish. Both waters are rich in aquatic life.

Visiting fishermen find Smith Creek's hospitality as rewarding as its fishing. Home-style cooking and family-style dining are available. Also, the ranch house has three bedrooms to accommodate singles and couples. After only one year

Facing Page: The new six-surface-acre trout pond at Smith Creek Ranch holds trophy size rainbow trout.

of operation Smith Creek has become a well known Nevada destination. For more information and bookings call (702) 423-4254 and ask for Diane from 8:00 a.m. to 5:00 p.m., Monday through Friday, or write Smith Creek Ranch, 570 N. Downs Ln. Fallon, NV 89406.

Willow Creek Pond

Willow Creek is on the south slope of Antler Peak at the 5,600-foot elevation. Actually there are two ponds. The bigger pond is roughly nine surface acres like Groves Lake. Originally the ponds were a water supply for mining and ranching. During 1960, the Division of Wildlife began a trout stocking program for local anglers. Today the ponds see most of their use right after the hatchery truck leaves, but some rainbows manage to remain. Upstream is a population of wild brook trout and there is a self-sustaining brown trout population. In May 1982, Willow Creek Pond gave up an 8-pound, 11-ounce brown trout.

Fly fishermen will appreciate the pond's remote location. They will also like the rich aquatic life, like mayflies, caddisflies, water boatmen, damselflies, dragonflies and blackflies. Don't forget the midge patterns early in the year.

To reach Willow Creek Pond take Nevada Highway 305 from either Interstate 80 or U.S. Highway 50. Roughly 12 miles south of Battle Mountain a

Wild brook trout bring fly fishermen to Nevada's remote waters.

blacktop road turns west from the highway. Take this turn. Within three miles the blacktop ends and graded gravel roads begin. Look for the Bureau of Land Management signs. Basically, it is a right turn from the paved road and then a northerly seven-mile drive to the ponds.

Camping is primitive at Willow Creek Pond. However, Battle Mountain is close by.

Toiyabe Mountains (Lander County)

The Toiyabe Range is one of nine Nevada mountain ranges with one or more peaks over 11,000 feet tall. Three Toiyabe peaks have this distinction and another five reach more than 10,000 feet. These mountains draw a thin, 50-mile-long line through the center of the Silver State.

Along the east flank is the Big Smokey Valley. A broad and arid expanse of desert, this valley absorbs the run off from the Toiyabe and Toquima ranges. Nevada Highway runs north and south through the Big Smokey connecting U.S. Highways 50 and 6.

To the west is the Reese River Valley. Improved graded dirt roads lead from U.S. Highway 50 south to Yomba Indian Reservation and beyond. It is possible, during dry weather, to drive all the way to Tonopah on these roads.

Only four Toiyabe Range streams are described here under Lander County. For more information about other streams and rivers see Chapter 13: Nye County.

Big Creek

Take the Reese River Road from Austin south 11 miles to reach this creek. Go another mile to reach the Forest Service Campground. The road is well maintained during all but the worst weather.

Big Creek is almost 10 miles long and mostly within the Toiyabe National Forest. The creek begins at the 8,400-foot elevation on the west side of the Toiyabes and flows west toward the Reese River. Brown trout, up to 870 fish per mile, live in Big Creek. Most fish average close to six inches because the creek has little good holding water in the form of pools. Still, some 10-inch fish are taken most seasons.

Fly fishermen will appreciate the light to moderate bank cover. The dense vegetation is downstream from the campground and this is also where most of the brown trout live.

Insect life is reasonably abundant in Big Creek. Stoneflies, mayflies, caddis-flies and blackflies make up most of the aquatic insects. Grasshoppers provide a tempting meal during the fall.

Birch Creek

Brown trout also live in Birch Creek. The last stream survey estimated the trout population between 180 to 2,000 fish per mile. Most of the fish captured during the survey averaged close to four inches. But some also reached the 12-inch size.

Birch Creek is east of Austin and south of Highway 50 roughly three miles. Turn west at the green and white sign onto a two-wheel-drive dirt road. This road parallels the main fork up to the 7,580-foot elevation and all of the north fork.

The main fork of Birch Creek is over eight miles long. Another three miles of fishing is available on the north fork. This is, however, a small mountain stream. Birch Creek averages four feet wide and three inches deep. Streamside willows and wild rose increase as the elevation increases.

Kingston Creek

Kingston Creek is the most popular stream in the Toiyabe Range. Anglers only need visit this stream once to understand why. Located 23 miles southeast of Austin, Kingston is nine miles long. Much of the stream meanders through broad meadows above and below Groves Lake. This is a favorite stream for fly fishermen.

In the narrow portions of the canyon the banks are protected by willows, wild rose and chokecherry. Close to the stream the pine, aspen and mountain mahogany make this a beautiful oasis in the desert.

At times, and depending on elevation, Kinsgton holds brown trout, rainbow trout and brook trout. Most recently brown trout dominate the stream.

Stoneflies don't show up in stream samples, at least not near the meadows. However, caddisflies, mayflies and blackflies are abundant. Scuds live in Groves Lake and also in weed beds downstream from the lake.

Camping at Kingston is the same as described under Groves Lake. The Forest Service Campground fills quickly over three-day weekends.

From Austin go east on U.S. 50 and turn south on Nevada 376. The Kingston turn is marked by a green and white highway sign.

Mill Creek

Mill Creek is not in the Toiyabe National Forest. This stream is located 21 miles south of Battle Mountain where it crosses Nevada Highway 305. An improved dirt road provides access to the main stream. Eighteen miles long, 14 miles of the creek crosses public land.

Fly fishermen will appreciate Mill Creek. Though there are few quality pools, streamside vegetation will not hamper casting. Stoneflies, mayflies and caddisflies provide fish forage and most popular patterns will catch fish.

During the 1984 stream survey, biologists found brook trout and brown trout. Brook trout in the upper stream were estimated at 230 fish per mile. These brookies average a respectable 8 1/2 inches. Downstream the browns numbered 11 fish per mile, but average close to 12 inches long.

Facing Page: Kingston Creek is a popular Nevada fishery because of its accessibility.

CHAPTER 11: White Pine County

Central Nevada's major east-west route is U.S. Highway 50. A *Life* magazine article dubbed it America's Loneliest Highway several decades back, but it remains the shortest route across the state. Mountain men Jedediah Smith and Howard Egan were the first white men to use the central route in the 1820s. Later, the Pony Express and the transcontinental telegraph would use the same route.

The eastern end of Nevada's portion of Highway 50 crosses White Pine County. The county had a brush with the boom and bust of gold and silver mining, but copper was the mineral that built the area's wealth. The copper boom ebbed recently. Now Magma Mining is re-working the Ruth copper pit.

Anglers and hunters both look to White Pine for some of the state's better fishing and hunting opportunities. It is a little remote from the rest of the state, but it is that very quality that adds to its attraction. While fishing in White Pine anglers can log a few miles, but the variety in scenery makes the drive worthwhile.

Along the southern end of the county the land changes. Instead of the streams flowing into the Great Basin, Nevada's geographical bowl, water runs out. The White River is the first indication of the change. It flows (when there is enough water) south toward Las Vegas and eventually into the Colorado River and on to the Sea of Cortez.

Bassett Lake

Many anglers visiting White Pine County will opt to pass Bassett Lake. This is a small, 75-surface-acre, warm water fishery on private land. Bassett is a day-use largemouth bass and northern pike fishing hole. In August 1988, Bassett produced a 25-pound pike.

This is a marsh-like reservoir that backs up creeks flowing west and south from the Schell Creek Mountains. An abundance of rooted aquatic plants provide cover for the fish and a challenge for anglers. Insect life, however, is prolific. Damselflies hatch in clouds of blue-bodied adults. Chironomids outnumber the damsels and are available to fish year-round—except during ice-covered winters. Bassett also has a good population of crayfish.

Two green signs with white lettering along the west side of U.S. 93 mark the two roads leading to Bassett Lake. The southern route is the easiest drive, and is approximately eight miles north of Ely. The northern access is north of McGill.

A long dike on the west end has a road that connects Bassett's north and south shores. There is an unimproved boat ramp available for lightweight trailered boats. Launching trailered craft, however, is dependent on water levels. Car-top boats and canoes can launch relatively easily. Float tubes and pontoon boats will find good access along the northern bank.

Cave Lake

Likely White Pine's most popular fishery, Cave Lake supports between 25,000 and 30,000 angler days per year. Stocked rainbow trout are the main attraction, but the lake also holds some very large and reclusive brown trout too. A few small browns are landed occasionally, but the big browns elude even experienced local anglers and visitors. Every brown over 15 or 16 inches that the local biologist has examined had another fish in its stomach.

The average rainbow trout measures near 11 inches at Cave Lake. The range is from nine to 20 inches. Big rainbows are hatchery brood stock moved to the lake. Some planted trout winter-over, but Cave Lake does not have a large forage base for trout. This is a classic put-and-take reservoir.

Rooted aquatic vegetation is more prevalent near the inlet. Midges provide the most important food source, but there are damselflies, mayflies, snails and

Cave Lake is one of Nevada's most popular State Parks. Fishing is a major attraction.

crayfish too. Most fishermen prefer to cast from shore, but Cave Lake is just right for a float tube or small boat.

Cave Lake is small at 32 surface acres, but it is 58 feet deep. The lake drops three to four feet every year due to downstream irrigation. Nevada's Division of Wildlife purchased the lake and the surrounding land in 1968. Today the State Parks Department operates two campgrounds and an improved boat ramp.

The Cave Lake Campground is just north of the lake. This campground has 36 improved sites with running water, flush toilets and showers. Elk Flat Campground is closer to Highway 93 and has 15 camp sites. Primitive camping is allowed beyond the pavement north of Cave Lake.

Getting to Cave Lake is easy, except after heavy winter snowstorms. Take U.S. Highways 50 and 93 (they run together) for seven miles south of Ely. Two large signs point to the east turn to Cave Lake. The road is paved all the way to the lake's upper end. However, winter ice fishing access is kept open by snow plows. Crews must plow the highways before worrying about the Cave Lake road.

Cold Creek Reservoir

In the northwest corner of White Pine County lies a small reservoir with good angling possibility. The dam leaks, however and maximum pool is held only for short periods. In recent years only the middle pond, Cold Creek has three ponds, has held water. The lower pond has not been able to hold water though it is the main reservoir.

The land Cold Creek is on is both privately-owned and Bureau of Land Management land. The Division of Wildlife and the BLM are trying to work with the new landowner to improve the fishery. At one time, the BLM wanted to build a campground at the lake.

Cold Creek has the ability to support a good trout population. It has been stocked regularly since 1972 and 16- to 22-inch rainbows have been landed.

Aquatic vegetation can reach nuisance levels during low-water periods. However, that same plant life supports abundant insects that allow trout to grow rapidly. Midges, mayflies, damselflies, dragonflies, scuds and tui chubs form the trouts' protein base.

Cold Creek Reservoir is located on the eastern slope of the Diamond Range and flows toward Newark Valley. The reservoir is 34 miles north of U.S. Highway 50 and 96 miles from Ely. A sign on Highway 50 marks the turn. Another route is from Jiggs, Nevada on the west slope of the Ruby Mountains. Rather than turning to take Harrison Pass to the Ruby Marsh, continue south 45 miles to Cold Creek Reservoir.

Even the big boys have to come out and eat sometime as this five-pound rainbow proves.

Comins Lake

"Easy to reach" and "big trout" are phrases used to describe Comins Lake. Comins, however, is on private land and the owner has not agreed to maintain a minimum pool.

The 382-surface-acre lake is formed by a realignment of U.S. Highway 93 just seven miles south of Ely. Comins is only 14 feet deep and 75 percent of the reservoir is between seven and 14 feet deep. Around the north end, the lake averages 12 feet deep. Almost two miles long, the lake is between half-mile and 375 feet wide.

Because the landowner permits public access for fishing and boating, Nevada anglers have a unique fishing opportunity. Comins is a very productive fishery due to its shallow, marsh-like nature. An abundance of rooted aquatic plants supply the basis for the up to 1 1/2 inches per month trout growth rate. Scuds, mayflies, damselflies, dragonflies, midges and snails turn the plants into trout protein.

Rainbow trout dominate the game fish population. Brown trout, last stocked in 1985, were likely lost when the lake was emptied during the recent drought. Wildlife biologists re-stocked Comins during the fall of 1995. Both species fit the football-trout definition perfectly. Comins Lake is in the Nevada Trophy Record book with a 13-pound, 8-ounce brown and a 5-pound, 14-ounce rainbow.

Though the landowner permits fishing access, no camping is available. This is not a problem, however, as Ely is seven miles to the north and Cave Lake State Park is seven miles east.

Illipah Reservoir

Another privately-owned irrigation reservoir, Illipah came under management as a public fishery in 1981. The state of Nevada built a new dam enlarging the reservoir capacity and guaranteeing a minimum pool of 160 acre feet. During low water the old dam's foundation almost divides the reservoir in two.

In its first good water year after the most recent drought, Illipah Creek had a less-than-exceptional water year. Still, the creek's volume was higher than seen in the previous seven or eight years. Illipah filled during the winter of 1995 to 1996, but the reservoir is subject to drawdowns for irrigation.

During 1995 creel checks, fisheries officials say anglers caught fish measuring 14 to 16 inches. This report was personally confirmed that August.

The upper lake is shallower than the new, lower lake. As a result, the aquatic plant life is thicker in the upper lake. If water quality and quantity is maintained, trout prefer the upper lake. During 1995, fishermen reported seeing brown trout feeding on schools of stocked rainbows.

Insect life at Illipah is typical of most reservoirs. Midges offer year-round protein until ice covers the surface. Mayflies, damselflies and dragonflies appear spring through fall. There are no minnows or rough fish in the reservoir according to the fisheries studies.

Illipah Reservoir's turnoff from U.S. Highway 50 is 36 miles west of Ely. From here a hard surface dirt road leads to the reservoir and a Bureau of Land Management Recreation Site. Campsites have wooden fences to provide a wind break, trash collection area, portable toilets, but no running water.

Silver Creek Reservoir

Silver Creek Reservoir lies within the shadows of 13,061-foot Wheeler Peak. Look on the eastern slope of the Snake Range two miles north of the junction of U.S. Highway 50 and State Route 487. Don't look for a sign marking the turn, in the summer of 1995 there wasn't one. The turn is roughly 55 miles east of Ely and seven miles west of the Utah border.

Silver Creek originates on 10,000-foot Mount Moriah. This is yet another irrigation reservoir. The dam's design almost guarantees a non-withdrawable minimum pool. At 15 surface acres and a maximum depth of 20 feet, Silver Creek is a small reservoir. During 1993, a flash flood carried a large amount of silt into the reservoir. It has been dredged since then, thanks to the Baker family and is fishable.

Most of the reservoir's brown trout were lost during the flood. Over time, upstream fish will migrate to the reservoir. A self-sustaining population of brown trout will again live in the reservoir along with stocked rainbows. Silver Creek's claim to angling fame is a 26-inch, 11-pound, 4-ounce brown trout.

A little shade is available as riparian vegetation is made up of cottonwood trees, willows, wild rose and tamarisk. Aquatic plants prove a nuisance during low-water years, but are limited to small areas at other times.

In addition to the typical still water food sources, Silver Creek has a fair population of crayfish. Scuds introduced into the lake, however, did not take.

Schell Creek Mountains

Most of the Schell Creek Range lies within a long, narrow piece of the Humboldt National Forest. Schell Creek, like so many Nevada mountains, runs north and south. Ely and Steptoe Valley lie along the range's western flank and Spring Valley is on the east.

U.S. Highway 50 crosses the range at Connors Pass 26 miles south of Ely. U.S. 93 runs north from Ely and intersects with Nevada 486 north of McGill. Highway 486 climbs the Duck Creek Range two miles north of McGill and exits again near Cave Lake and Comins Lake seven miles south of Ely. Nevada Highway 893 cuts north through Spring Valley east of Connors Pass and north of U.S. Highway 50. Twenty-two miles north of Highway 50, Nevada 893 becomes a hard surface dirt road.

The north end of the Schell Creek Range has two roads. One is a four-wheel-drive road that crosses the mountains east of McGill. This route follows Kalamazoo Creek on the east slope. An easier, if not dustier, drive is the graded gravel road that turns east from U.S. 93, 22 miles north of McGill. Eventually, this road reaches the dirt road version of Nevada 893 and continues east to the Goshute Indian Reservation on the Utah border.

All the streams listed below are accessible by one or more of these routes. In fact, most of the streams in the Schell Creek Range have trout in them.

Cleve Creek

Cleve Creek is an east slope stream. Take Nevada 893 north from Majors Place approximately 11 miles. Leave the pavement by turning west toward the Bureau of Land Management Campground on Cleve Creek. The camping is primitive, but it has vault toilets.

Most of the stream's 8 1/2 miles is within the forest boundary, but almost two miles is BLM land. Access is by dirt road along the main branch and on foot to the north fork.

In 1984, a stream survey estimated Cleve's combined brown and rainbow trout population at as high as 535 fish per mile. Some trout were in the 12-inch range, but the average was 6 1/4 inches. The same survey recorded moderate streamside cover consisting of willow, wild rose and current. Tall timber grows above this creek's 6,650-foot beginning.

Cleve Creek's trout food includes stoneflies, mayflies, caddisflies and worms.

Duck Creek

Turn right onto Nevada Highway 486 from U.S. 93 north of McGill to reach the fishable portion of Duck Creek. This stream, during wet years, flows almost all the way to Elko County. Nevada anglers, however, concentrate on the upper stream in the valley between the Schell Creek and Duck Creek ranges.

Here the stream meanders through an open valley occasionally dotted with willows. For five miles above the confluence with Berry Creek, anglers can cast to mostly brown trout and maybe a few rainbows and brookies. During 1985's stream survey, the trout population was put at 392 fish per mile. Fly fishermen will enjoy this section of Duck Creek. The fish are not big by other White Pine County standards, but prove a challenge. Stoneflies don't live in the meadow portion of the stream. However, caddis and Diptera are common. Also look for mayfly hatches.

Big Indian Creek

Big Indian is north of McGill approximately 15 miles, where it crosses U.S. Highway 93. Access is excellent and the scenery borders on spectacular. During dry weather a two-wheel-drive vehicle with good ground clearance can make the drive. The road goes beyond the stream's headwaters, into the Humboldt Forest and near the top of the mountain range.

Only three miles of stream are considered fishable, however. Big Indian is typical of the small streams in White Pine County. It does hold populations of brook trout and rainbow trout. This stream is included for anglers willing to do a little exploring.

Kalamazoo Creek

Another east slope stream, Kalamazoo is 66 miles up Spring Valley from U.S. Highway 50. A shorter four-wheel-drive route from Nevada 486 is available, but only true off-road anglers will appreciate the drive. The fishable portion of the stream's North Fork is accessible by the unimproved road called Faun Trail. Spell that four-wheel-drive.

Brown trout are the dominant sport fish in Kalamazoo. Most of the trout live above the forest boundary. In the main stream below the forest, the brown trout population is estimated at nearly 900 fish per mile. Below the confluence with the North Fork of Kalamazoo, the population estimate jumps to over 1,175 fish per mile. More fishing is available downstream, including in the diversion ditch.

Birch and cottonwood offer the stream moderate cover in the lower elevations. Farther up the drainage, aspen and white furs shade the stream. Fly fishermen, however, will find the stream fishable though occasionally challenging.

A good brown trout fishery, Kalamazoo has stoneflies, mayflies, caddisflies, blackflies and scuds.

McCoy Creek

Only five miles long, most of McCoy Creek passes through Forest Service land. Turn west from Spring Valley's Nevada Highway 893 onto an unimproved dirt road that is marked with a brown and white BLM sign that was last seen hanging by one screw. The upper stream is accessible only on foot.

In 1995, McCoy Creek's brown trout were estimated at over 832 fish per mile. A good population for a small stream, even if the average was only 7 1/4 inches long. Brown trout prefer the lower creek and reach the 10-inch mark. Upstream rainbows can grow as long as nine inches.

A wildfire burned the majority of the land around the lower creek. Dominant vegetation today includes willows, water birch, wild rose and grass. Still the stream has abundant numbers of caddisflies, stoneflies and mayflies. There are also some freshwater worms in the creek.

McCoy has excellent pools and cascades over boulders and logs. A pipeline diversion presents a barrier to the trouts' upstream movement.

Piermont Creek

A little more than eight miles north of McCoy Creek is Piermont Creek. Piermont is almost seven miles long and has quality pools for the stream's brown trout. In 1984, the browns were estimated at 675 per mile with an average length over eight inches.

Terrain is heavily forested above the forest boundary. Aspens, water birch and wild rose shelter the length of the creek.

The food source for browns includes stoneflies, mayflies, caddisflies and blackflies.

Steptoe Creek

Most White Pine creeks present a challenge to fly fishermen. Huge willows, small trees, sage brush and wild rose wait to grab flies and shred leaders. Steptoe Creek is such a stream.

Dapping—reaching over or around the brush and gently dropping a fly on the water—is a good approach. Still fly fishermen can cast if they adjust their tackle. Hand-tied leaders measuring three feet long and tapered to 4X tippets do the trick. Enough fly line is outside the rod tip to allow for easy handling when dapping or casting. The tippet is light enough to cast or dap a small dry fly such as a Blonde Humpy.

Wild brown and rainbow trout in Steptoe use the streamside vegetation as cover from predators. A well placed fly drifted near or under the overhanging cover brings solid strikes. In addition to good riparian habitat, the stream has good pools for trout and plenty of riffles for the insects trout eat. The biggest fish is about 10 inches, which is just right for this small stream.

Steptoe follows the dirt road portion of Nevada 486 down to Cave Lake Park. From the park, the creek and the pavement continue down to Highway 50 and Comins Lake.

A popular and easily accessible stream, the wild trout would soon be fished-out if the Division of Wildlife didn't stock some fish.

Tailings Creek

This creek is a good reason to turnoff toward Bassett Lake. The fishable section of Tailings Creek is only about two miles long, but it is fun fly fishing.

How much fun? Tailings is in the Nevada record book for a 3-pound, 2-ounce brook trout, a 7-pound, 5-ounce brown trout and a 5-pound, 6-ounce rainbow. Occasionally, pike from Bassett show up in the creek too.

Tailings Creek is a spring-fed stream that pops up on the west side of the big pile of mine waste or tailings at McGill. Turn west from U.S. Highway 93 onto the southern access to Bassett Lake near the Old Club 50. Cross the railroad tracks and look to the right for parking.

Timber Creek

Timber Creek is a small west slope stream that is diverted by a pipeline high in the mountains. There is a small self-sustaining population of rainbows in the creek, however.

During the last official survey, the fishable length of Timber Creek was 1.3 miles. Portions of the stream are bushy, but this is not steep terrain.

The Forest Service has a campground near the end of the road. A Girl Scout Campground is located nearby.

Snake Range

The Snake Range is a range of mountains southeast of the Schell Creek Mountains. Like the Schell Creek Range, the Snake Range lies within the Checkerboard boundaries of the Humboldt National Forest. Unlike the Schell Creek Range, the Snake Range is home to America's youngest national park. Within its boundaries are the Lehman Caves National Monument and five fishable small streams. One stream leaves Forest Service land and crossess U.S. Highway 50 west of Nevada Highway 487. North of U.S. 50 and the small community of Baker, Nevada is still another fishable stream.

Lehman Caves is just one attraction featured in Great Basin National Park and the Snake Range.

The streams listed here are all east slope water. Access from Ely is via U.S. 50 to Nevada 487 near Baker. This is the way to the park entrance. Highway 487 becomes Utah Highway 21 seven miles southeast of Baker.

The park and the caves are a must-stop for anglers traveling this portion of the sagebrush sea. Ragged alpine peaks, 13,063-foot Wheeler Peak and ancient bristlecone pines add to the area's attraction.

Baker Creek

Baker Creek begins at 10,080 feet on the eastern flank of the Snake Range inside Great Basin National Park. Inside the park, anglers have two campgrounds to choose from along Baker creek. Gray Cliffs is a primitive campground located at 7,000 feet in a steep canyon portion of the stream's drainage. Baker Creek Campground is located above 7,500 feet on an improved gravel road. Here the alder, aspen, willow and wild rose combine to help separate the 34 campsites. This campground has vault toilets and running water.

Few fish live above the Baker Creek Trailhead. This does not mean trout won't move upstream when conditions permit. During a 1990 stream survey, the combined brown, brook and rainbow trout population was estimated at 776 fish per mile. The average size was a respectable 8.6 inches. These are wild trout. Planting hatchery fish is not permitted in our national parks.

While aspen, willow and cottonwood dominate upper-elevation vegetation, the plant life thins considerably downstream. The creek begins moving away from the main road below Gray Cliffs Campground. Below the cliffs, sagebrush slowly becomes the prevalent streamside plant as Baker flows into Lehman Creek. Fly fishermen will find enough tall plants to keep them watching their back cast, but not enough to leave the rod in the car.

Lehman Creek

A paved road, three campgrounds and a trailhead leading to the bristlecone pines and ice fields, make Lehman Creek popular. Brook, brown and rainbow trout add an extra attraction for anglers.

Lower Lehman Creek Campground has 11 sites among the aspens. Upper Lehman Creek Campground has 24 sites mostly for tent campers. Wheeler Peak Campground has 37 sites sitting at 10,000 feet above sea level. All have running water and pit toilets.

Brook trout dominate the upper elevation of Lehman Creek. Not many fish, however, are found above 9,000 feet. Closer to Upper Lehman Campground anglers find rainbows. Browns are found closer to Lower Lehman Campground and the confluence with Baker Creek.

A good system of trails parallels most of the creek; add the road and anglers have excellent access. Remember, however, this is not a stocked stream. Finding more and bigger fish usually means getting away from other fishermen and the developed areas.

Outside the park, Lehman Creek loses much of the habitat that supports trout. Depending on water flows, fish live outside the park, but their numbers begin to decline.

Silver Creek

At U.S. Highway 50's junction with Nevada 487 turn north onto a dirt road. This is the same road that leads to Silver Creek Reservoir. Silver Creek itself is 15 miles long and the entire stream above the reservoir runs through public land. The creek originates at the 9,000-foot elevation and flows into Silver Creek Reservoir. A dirt road paralleled the upper creek until flooding blew out part of the road. However, a four-wheel-drive road enters the headwater area from Miller Basin.

Bankside cover is sparse. Willows and currant provide the most shade and trout protection. Bank stability is poor below irrigation diversions. The stream suffered a flash flood in 1993 that deposited a lot of silt into the reservoir below.

Brown trout do, however, live in Silver Creek and the stream is fishable. In fact, the stream supports natural trout reproduction. In 1984, the trout population was estimated at 1,267 trout per mile. The average size, however, is a small 6 1/2 inches. Some 10-inch fish were found. Brook trout inhabit the upper reaches of Silver Creek. The browns stay in the lower elevations. Rainbow trout, which live in tributary streams, also make their way into the creek.

Silver Creek has abundant populations of insects. Blackflies, caddisflies and mayflies inhabit most of the stream. As time allows nature to recover from the flash flood, Silver Creek should harbor more trout like those found during the 1984 stream survey.

Snake Creek

South of Baker, Nevada, just before Nevada Highway 487 crosses into Utah, a dirt road leads to Snake Creek. A good road at the lower elevations, it can turn nasty during storms and spring run-off, especially at upper elevations. The road follows the entire length of the stream. Look for the sign pointing to the Spring Creek Fish Rearing Station.

Snake Creek starts at the 9,280-foot elevation and flows east to the 5,340-foot elevation Snake Valley. Within Nevada, 13 1/2 miles of the stream are accessible.

Dense growths of willow, wild rose and cottonwood dominate the upstream vegetation. The density of streamside vegetation decreases as the elevation decreases. Mayflies, caddisflies, blackflies and stoneflies inhabit most of Snake Creek.

Snake Creek has the best fishing in the Snake Range. Brown trout occasionally reach and even top the 10-inch mark, but the average is closer to six inches. Population estimates in 1990 were 761 brown trout per mile. Above the pipeline, which acts as a fish barrier, most trout are brookies. Below the pipe, anglers cast for brown trout and escaped rainbows.

Strawberry Creek

North of Great Basin National Park and south of U.S. 50, Strawberry Creek flows north and east. After crossing Highway 50 roughly seven miles from Sacramento Pass it turns east. Access is by dirt road from U.S. Highway 50 at Baker Highway Maintenance Station.

Seven miles of the upper stream is considered fishable. Flows become too intermittent at lower elevations to support trout year in and year out. Primitive camping is available within the Great Basin Park. Access is good and the scenery alone makes the trip worthwhile.

Cover for the fish and stream consists of moderate stands of willow, wild rose and waterbirch. Also, the creek has several beaver dams. Food sources include stoneflies, mayflies and caddisflies.

Brook trout populations are estimated at 158 fish per mile. Some hybrid rainbow-cutthroat trout are in the stream, too.

Weather close to the 10,000-foot origin of Strawberry Creek can be cold and wet, so come prepared.

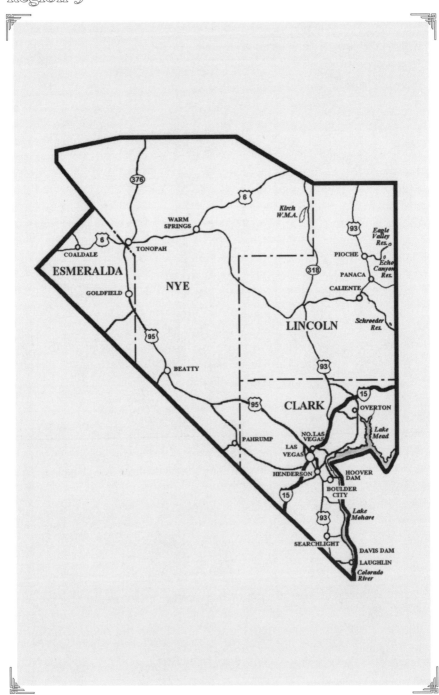

Region 3

Following is a little trivia for the campfire from *The Nevada Trivia Book* by Richard Moreno. Nye County covers 18,294 square miles, which makes it the third largest in America. Sixty-three percent of Nevada's residents live in Clark County and Las Vegas is the biggest city in the state. Las Vegas receives only four inches of moisture a year. Yet the residents use 375 gallons of water per person per day, more than any other American city.

Region 3 is the driest area in Nevada. Most of the fishing is around the geographical edges of the region. Northern Nye, eastern Lincoln, southern Clark and western Esmeralda counties are described here. Some of the waters can produce exciting fishing. Fishing in the area's state parks is supported with stocked fish, but a few hold-overs get pretty big.

Fishermen use Interstate 15 near Las Vegas and U.S. Highways 95 and 93. When traveling east-west, U.S. Highway 6 runs between Tonopah and Ely just north of the Nevada Test Site.

Las Vegas, Henderson and Tonopah are the area's biggest cities. Traveling fishermen can find the services they need in these communities. Specialty stores catering to anglers only exist around Las Vegas.

CHAPTER 12: Esmeralda County

Nevada's least populated county and likely its least fished, is Esmeralda County. Like much of the state, mining and ranching form the economic backbone of this southwestern county. The county's claim to fame was the gold mining boom during the early 1900s at Goldfield. In 1904, Virgil Earp, brother of the famous Wyatt Earp, moved to Goldfield. He would become a deputy sheriff for Esmeralda County and die in Goldfield in 1905.

Today a new mining boom has taken hold. Most of the county's residents, however, work at ranching, maintaining highways, or at the Nevada Test Site. For anglers this means services like food, gas and tackle are limited. Tonopah, which straddles the Esmeralda and Nye County line and Goldfield are the biggest towns.

U.S. 95 drops south from Hawthone and Walker Lake to merge with U.S. Highway 6 west of Tonopah. From here U.S. 95 regains its identity as it turns south again on its solitary trip to Las Vegas. U.S. Highway 6 is the east-west road. From Tonopah, it goes west into Mineral County and California. Good blacktop county roads allow access on the east flank of the White Mountains.

Chiatovich Creek

Singling out Chiatovich as the only stream in Esmeralda County does not mean every angler should or will stop and fish. If, however, exploring new country and fishing new water fuels whatever sends you fishing, put Chiatovich on your list.

Located on the west flank of the White Mountains, two miles of this stream is in California. The remaining 13 miles of fishable water is all Nevada's. A small creek, Chiatovich averages five feet wide and six inches deep. The stream starts at 11,700 feet above sea level and enters Nevada at the 9,675-foot elevation. It holds good numbers of trout, however.

Brook trout are estimated at 105 fish per mile and rainbow trout number 400 per mile. Fishing pressure from the middle fork to the highway is above average for area streams. Above the middle fork, angling pressure declines due to spring flooding and locked gates. Beyond the gates marking private land are bad roads or no roads.

Chiatovich grows good numbers of mayflies and caddisflies. Thick stands of willow will keep fly fishermen away from the lower stream. Adventurous fly anglers, however, will enjoy the scenery and fishing in the upper elevations.

Go east from Tonopah 44 miles on U.S. Highway 6 and turn south on Nevada 773. Nine miles farther is the junction of Nevada Highway 264. Continue south six miles to Chiatovich Creek and turn west on the main dirt road. The road is marked with a brown BLM sign most years. From here the road climbs out of Fish Lake Valley and up the east slope of the White Mountains. Primitive campsites are available along the lower creek.

Alpine fishing is often a solitary experience for anglers willing to make the trip.

CHAPTER 13: Nye County

Is it coincidence that Nye County is shaped like a mushroom cloud? During the 1860s, Nevada's founders could not have predicted the atomic age or the Nevada Test Site. Nuclear testing, however, is not Nye County's only claim to national fame. Within the borders of the Nellis Air Force Range is the mystery base known as Groom Lake. Its secret military research and testing operations have helped fuel stories about extraterrestrial sightings and more.

Ranchers in central Nevada, Nye County most recently, have challenged the federal government's authority to administer public lands. Called the Sagebrush Rebellion, the issue remains a smoldering hot spot in area politics.

For Nevada anglers, however, Nye County is an important area. The northern part of the county includes the Toiyabe and Monitor Mountains. Along the eastern portion of the county is the Kirch Wildlife Management area and four very fishable reservoirs.

Within Nevada's largest county, it is a long drive to the fishing. U.S. Highway 6 crosses from east to west, or Ely to Tonopah. U.S. Highway 95 skirts around all the military reserve land as it passes through Esmeralda County and then through Nye. Tonopah is the only community of substantial size in this central Nevada county.

Cherry Creek

South and west of Ely are the Quinn Canyon and Grant Mountain ranges. Both lie within the boundary of the Humboldt National Forest. Cherry Creek heads from the east side of the Quinn Canyon Range and flows into Garden Valley south of Kirch Wildlife Management Area. The taller Grant Range has five peaks over 10,000 feet that add to the scenery, but not the stream.

Of Cherry Creek's 28-mile length, all but 7 1/2 miles are on public land. A small stream, the creek averages 4.3 feet wide and close to three inches deep. Rainbow trout dominate Cherry Creek and Little Cherry Creek. During sustained wet years, they can number close to 1,000 fish per mile. In the lower elevations, brown trout begin showing up too. All the trout average close to seven inches long, but a few bigger fish live here, too.

Abundant trout food is available in the form of mayflies, caddisflies, blackflies, midges and scuds. Fly fishermen will find dense streamside vegetation in the lower elevations during good water years. Upstream, shade is provided by willows and cottonwood trees. The stream's drainage is a piñon pine forest.

Cherry Creek is 73 road miles southwest of Lund and 165 road miles east of Tonopah. Or take U.S. Highway 6 from Ely 17 miles and turn south onto Nevada Highway 318. Drive 32 miles south and take the Sunnyside dirt road. Continue past Kirch Wildlife Managment area approximately 25 miles when the graded gravel road leaves Garden Valley to climb Cherry Creek Summit. This is a two-wheel-drive road during dry weather, but can turn into a four-wheel-drive road when wet. A campground and picnic area is available just upstream from the canyon mouth.

Wayne A. Kirch Wildlife Management Area

Like most of Nevada's Wildlife Management Areas, Kirch's water is maintained primarily for waterfowl. As a result, this is a wetland or swamp-like environment. Still there are four places anglers can fish.

Fishermen visiting Kirch have a few extra rules to follow. For example, vehicle traffic is limited to protect wildlife. Camping in the wildlife area is restricted to two campgrounds.

Boats must follow Nevada's other regulations and limit their speed to five nautical miles per hour. Boat launches include floating docks within narrow channels.

While casting a Woolly Bugger from his boat, Reno resident Terry Barron hooked and released many rainbow trout.

Parts of Kirch Wildlife Area are closed to trespassing. Fishermen using boats or float tubes will find buoys crossing portions of the waters described below. Please respect these boundaries.

Wayne A. Kirch Wildlife Management Area is located 70 miles south of Ely via U.S. Highway 6 and Nevada 318. From Las Vegas take Interstate 15 east and turn north on U.S. Highway 93. At Crystal Springs continue north on Nevada Highway 318. Look for the well marked turn to the Wildlife Area south of Sunnyside announcing Gap Mountain and Dave Deacon Campgrounds.

Dave Deacon Campground has tables and vault toilets. This campground's tall cottonwood trees are visible throughout most of the area. Gap Mountain Campground also has tables, vault toilets and a few lean-to style shelters.

Adams-McGill Reservoir

Like all the waters in Kirch Wildlife Area, Adams-McGill is in the old White River drainage. This is the biggest reservoir at 785 surface acres. The entire reservoir is shallow which contributes to thick aquatic weed growth and insect life. Much of the lower lake is made up of channels like Ruby Marsh. In fact, during the summer, weeds and mosquitoes discourage most anglers. Water temperatures range from the mid-70s during summer to freezing during the winter.

Largemouth bass are the primary sport fish and they average eight inches long with a 14-inch fish considered a trophy. In 1981, a 25 1/2-inch, 6-pound, 12-ounce rainbow was taken from this water. Rainbow no longer exist in this reservoir as the last prolonged drought did them in and Nevada no longer plants trout in Adams-McGill.

Cold Springs Reservoir

Rainbow trout still live in Cold Springs Reservoir. The largest fish checked by fisheries personnel during 1995 was a 25 1/2-inch, 8-pound, 4-ounce trophy. Trout in the 15- to 20-inch range are not unusual. Largemouth bass also inhabit this 275-surface-acre reservoir. Bass average close to 14 inches and 1 1/2 pounds, but a few 18-inch or bigger bass live here too. Bass are not stocked regularly, but rainbows are. Cold Springs is potentially the best fishery in the Wildlife Management Area.

Like Adams-McGill, aquatic weed growth restricts angling late in the summer. Some of the thickest weed growth is along the east side near the boat ramp.

Dacey Reservoir

This reservoir went dry during 1991 and 1992 to allow repairs to be done on the water control system and dam. Dacey is the western-most reservoir and is used as a surge reservoir. Still there is fishing available in this 185-surface-acre reservoir. It is, however, closed to fishing from February 15 through August 15 each year.

In 1993, largemouth bass from outside of Nevada were stocked in Dacey. As the water level stabilizes, the bass will begin spawning. It is not known, however, if trout will return to Dacey. During 1978, a 5-pound, 12-ounce Dacey Reservoir rainbow trout was entered in Nevada's Trophy Fish Program.

Haymeadow Reservoir

Haymeadow has 190 surface acres, but, like the other Wildlife Management Area reservoirs, it is shallow. Pond weed and watermilfoil frustrate late-summer fishermen but produce good numbers of insects.

Largemouth bass, rainbow trout and black bullhead catfish live in Haymeadow. Creel checks during 1993 show the trout averaged 13-inches-plus and the bass averaged 12 1/4 inches. Nevada's Trophy Fish Program records a six-pound rainbow taken in 1981 and a seven-pound brown landed in 1980. More fish are taken from float tubes and boats than from shore at Haymeadow.

Monitor Range

The Monitor Range is actually two mountain ranges east of the Toiyabe Range. Peaks in the Monitors are not as tall, nor is the terrain as steep, as the Toiyabes. Still there is fishing for those anglers with the desire to get away from the crowds. Two of the more popular streams are described here.

Access to the Monitor Range is via Monitor Valley on the range's western slope.

Barley Creek

Six miles of Barley Creek's 11-mile length is fishable. The stream averages eight feet wide and five inches deep. Barley Creek starts at the 9,300-foot elevation and flows into diversion canals at about 7,000 feet.

Brook trout average roughly 544 fish per mile, but they usually reach just over five inches. Brown trout populate Barley at 211 fish per mile and reach the seven-inch range. Rainbow trout only number 53 per mile, but can grow to the 10-inch range.

All of Barley Creek is on public land. Fly fishermen will find little in the way of brush to block their cast, but lots of insects to imitate. Water beetles, midges, a few stoneflies, mayflies and caddisflies are the available food for trout.

From Tonopah take U.S. Highway 6 east and turn north onto Nevada Highway 376. About 13 miles on this road turn northeast onto a graded gravel road that leads to the ghost town of Belmont. Upon reaching Belmont, some 27 miles later, turn east and cross the Monitor Valley some nine miles. BLM signs mark the way, but they have a habit of getting knocked down.

From Austin and U.S. Highway 50 turn south at the intersection of Nevada Highway 376. Take the long straight dirt road leading to the Toquima Range and Toquima Cave. After crossing the mountains turn south along the Monitor Valley toward Belmont. From Belmont turn east across the valley.

Primitive camping is available along the five miles of dirt road that parallels the stream. Hiking anglers will find several miles of stream to explore past the road's end.

Mosquito Creek

Fourteen miles due north of Barley Creek is Mosquito Creek. Another small stream, Mosquito averages three feet wide and just over two inches deep. Still there are six miles of fishable water where brook trout can reach 11 inches and rainbow trout top 10 inches.

Fly fishermen visiting Mosquito Creek must prepare for occasional dense stands of willows. Short leaders allow casting and dapping in the tight spaces. At the lower elevations, trout hide in the undercut banks. Mayflies, caddisflies (five species), blackflies and a few stoneflies make up the primary food source.

Mosquito Creek drains the upper reaches of Table Mountain. It starts at the 9,950-foot elevation and is diverted at the canyon mouth near the 6,900-foot elevation.

This creek is 62 miles north of Tonopah and 66 miles southeast of Austin. Three miles of dirt road parallels the stream. Only primitive camping is available.

Toiyabe Mountains (Nye County)

Within Nye County, this book describes four Toiyabe Range streams. Exploring anglers will find more. Five of the range's 10,000-foot and taller peaks lie within Nye County. These mountains catch a lot of winter snow. The resulting streams are some of the most underfished in the state.

East-flowing streams are accessed from Nevada Highway 376 and the Big Smoky Valley. Use the system of improved gravel roads south of U.S. Highway 50 and Austin to reach the west-flowing streams.

Reese River

The Reese River crosses U.S. Highway 50 some seven miles west of Austin. There is no fishing in this area as the river disappears into seeps. South of the highway much of the water is diverted for agriculture. An exceptionally wet winter recently kept the river flowing rapidly beyond Austin and U.S. Highway 1995, but those conditions are not common.

Much of the lower river is on private or reservation land. Access to the upper river, above the ranches and the Yomba Indian Reservation, is limited to hikers and horseback anglers.

Drive 28 1/2 miles south from U.S. 50 to reach fishable portions of the river. Another route is a 60-mile drive from Tonopah via Indian Valley.

In the remote areas fly fishermen will find light to heavy cover. About 50 percent of the bank cover is grass and 50 percent is brush. Active beaver colonies throughout the drainage add to the challenge.

Rainbow, hybrid bowcutts, brook and brown trout live in the Reese River. Rainbow are found throughout the drainage and average 465 fish per mile. Brook trout prefer higher elevations, close to the 8,760-foot origin and they average 190 fish per mile. Look for brown trout at lower elevations.

Cold, clear water makes this river a good trout fishery. Good numbers of mayflies, caddisflies, stoneflies, damselflies, scuds, snails and blackflies provide the forage. Don't forget to bring a few streamers as the river has a few rough fish too.

San Juan Creek

Twenty-seven miles south of U.S. Highway 50, turn off the Reese River Road to reach San Juan Creek. Private land limits access from the confluence of Cottonwood Creek to the forest boundary. A two-wheel-drive (during dry weather) road parallels the entire length of the stream including the south fork.

San Juan Creek is nine miles long, but only 7.6 miles is considered fishable including the south fork. The stream is small at an average of four feet wide and two inches deep. Still the stream holds rainbow trout.

Because of the easy access, San Juan is a put-and-take fishery. Nevada's Division of Wildlife stocks the stream regularly.

North Twin River

An east slope stream, this river is 70 road miles north of Tonopah and 20 miles northwest of Round Mountain. From Austin it is a 52-mile drive. A passable—four-wheel-drive recommended—road extends less than a half-mile above the mouth of the river canyon. Beyond this point only foot and horse traffic get through.

Six of the river's seven mile length is fishable. Small for a river, the North Twin averages three feet nine inches wide and three inches deep. About one mile below the confluence with South Twin River, the stream enters a three mile long gorge.

Primitive camping is available. Use the same places last fall's hunters and fishermen used.

The upper stream is good fishing for brook trout and rainbows in plunge pools and behind beaver dams. Brook trout number about 200 per mile and a few grow as long as 10 inches. Rainbow trout number 500 per mile and quite a few reach the 12-inch mark.

Fly fishermen will find open streambanks along the stream's higher elevations. The lower the elevation the thicker the streamside brush becomes. Use flies that imitate mayflies, caddisflies, stoneflies and blackflies. If visiting the river during fall bring grasshopper patterns.

South Twin River

The South Twin—yes, it is south of the North Twin—is one of the largest streams flowing east from the Toiyabe Range. A total of 13 1/2 miles long, the last five miles of river is diverted into a pipeline for irrigation. The South Fork of the South Twin is 4 1/2 miles long and the West Fork is 3.2 miles long. Including the tributaries, over 14 miles of the South Twin River is fishable.

Look for rainbow and brook trout in the South Twin. Rainbows up to 10 inches number roughly 252 fish per mile. Brook trout up to 10 inches average 130 fish per mile at upper elevations.

Open streambanks make for relatively easy fly casting on the South Twin River. Some willows and aspen grow along the stream banks in this piñon forest drainage.

Surprisingly, the South Twin sees heavy angler use for such a remote small stream.

CHAPTER 14: Lincoln County

Less than an hour from the glitter and crowds of Las Vegas, Lincoln County remains a remote cow-county. Fishermen driving north on U.S. Highway 93 from Vegas will notice a change in the color and texture of the land. More and more green shows against the stark hues of the desert. Also, the mountains get closer as the valleys the road follows narrow.

Anglers wanting to drive between Las Vegas and the Monitor or Toiyabe ranges should take Nevada Highway 375. Stop in the small town of Rachel at the A-Le-Inn (pronounced "alien") for a cold one and a little color. Stories abound about UFOs and visitors from outer space abound. Stay on U.S. Highway 93 to reach Caliente and Pioche, the county's biggest communities. Fishermen will find most of the services they need in these towns. This route takes anglers to the fishing described in this section.

Beaver Dam Wash

Beaver Dam Wash is a stream that begins in the Dixie National Forest of Utah. It enters Nevada in a gorge or narrow canyon. Water not used for irrigation flow back into Utah. Nearly nine miles of stream flow through Nevada, but only three miles are considered fishable. The fishable water starts at the state line and goes downstream to the confluence with Headwaters Wash. Beaver Dam averages five feet wide and two inches deep. Much of the fishable waters are within Beaver Dam State Park.

Turn east from U.S. 93 at Caliente to reach Beaver Dam Wash. The road is good graded gravel for 34 miles through the small settlement of Acoma. This road, however, gets very messy during wet weather and four-wheel-drive vehicles can get stuck. Slightly over one mile below Headwaters Wash confluence, the road crosses the creek and follows it. Below is private land.

Rainbow trout up to eight inches populate the stream Their numbers are estimated at 1,000 fish per mile. Fly fishermen will find them eating mayflies, caddisflies (five species), midges and snails. The wash also has some baitfish.

Schroeder Reservoir

Schroeder backs up Beaver Dam Wash within the state park. Fishermen access the reservoir the same way as the wash. A dirt road nears the stream at the north end of the park. From here it is an easy float down to the reservoir, or a short hike.

This is small water at 14 surface acres and 20 feet deep. Coontail grows thick along the northern shore limiting angler access. The reservoir's north end is the most used by fishermen.

Rainbow trout have been stocked in Schroeder since 1961. During 1993, the planted fish averaged 9 3/4 inches long. Upstream of the reservoir some small fish reproduce naturally. Downstream from the dam a few larger rainbows that escaped the reservoir are occasionally caught.

Eagle Valley Reservoir

Eagle Valley Reservoir is eighteen miles east of Pioche and U.S. 93 via Nevada Highway 322. Because the reservoir is located within Spring Valley State Park, anglers will find excellent boat launch and camping facilities. At 65 surface acres Eagle Valley is a popular fishery.

Brown trout were introduced at Eagle Valley as a biological control for rough fish. In 1994, some 3,500 browns were stocked. That same year some big browns were also caught. One fish measured 21 inches and weighed 5 pounds, 5 ounces. The one that made the record book was 26 3/4 inches long and weighed 9 pounds, 2 ounces. Over 52,022 rainbow trout are stocked in Eagle Valley too. Though the Trophy Fish Program does not have a rainbow entry for this reservoir, nice size rainbows are landed regularly.

Nevada normally stocks Eagle Valley from April through June and in October and November. This is when most of the crowds descend on the park.

Fly fishermen will find all of the normal stillwater insects to imitate. Since the old stream channel is over 25 feet deep and the reservoir is 48 feet deep near the dam, bring your sinking lines. Low oxygen levels, however, keep the trout from going too deep. Aquatic weeds can create access problems for float tubes in some areas.

Spring Valley State Park had 78,000 visitors in 1994. The 37 campsites with running water, showers and flush toilets fill fast. Overflow camping is available outside the park, including Eagle Valley Resort (702) 962-5293.

Echo Canyon Reservoir

South and slightly west of Eagle Valley Reservoir sits Echo Canyon Reservoir. Take Nevada Highway 322 east from Pioche and U.S. Highway 93. Twelve miles from town turn south eight miles to reach Echo Canyon State Park. Echo Canyon Park has the same facilities as Spring Valley State Park. The camping and boat ramp hold most interest for anglers, however. The 34 covered sites have the water turned on for the showers, etc. on April 15.

Also of interest to anglers are the rainbow trout, white crappie and large-mouth bass. During 1993, rainbows made up 22 1/2 percent of the fish population. White crappie and bass made up 38 3/34 percent and 37 1/2 percent of the fish population respectively. Again the Nevada Trophy Fish Program does not have a rainbow trout entry for Echo Canyon. A largemouth entry, however, measured 21 inches and weighed seven pounds. The white crappie entry came in at 14 inches and two pounds.

Volcanic rock forms the aqueduct leading to the reservoir. Built in 1969 in Meadow Valley Wash, this reservoir is a popular fishery for Las Vegas anglers. This 70-surface-acre lake has a maximum depth of 25 feet. An almost ideal warm-water fishery, Echo Canyon can give boating fishermen a bad time with aquatic weeds near shore. Float-tubing fly fishermen face the same challenge.

The lake can drop to very low levels during dry years. It is a good idea to check conditions first.

Pahranagat National Wildlife Refuge

Pronounced per-RANNA-gut, this wildlife refuge is located 83 miles north of Las Vegas on U.S. Highway 93. The refuge was established in 1964. It covers 5,380 acres of which 872 acres is wetlands. Of the wetlands, only 700 acres is open water.

Light lines and fine tippets make average size trout a challenge for skilled anglers.

Water quality and quantity plague fisheries management at Pahranagat. Largemouth bass were introduced in 1971. A record 9-pound, 7-ounce bass was landed in 1985. Occasionally fish over five pounds are caught, but the average size is closer to 12 inches. White crappie and black bullhead were first stocked in 1979.

Before 1984, Pahranagat was not known as a good bass fishery. During 1989, the reservoir was poisoned to remove carp. Restocking with Florida large-mouth bass and white crappie followed. Today Pahranagat produces fair fishing for crappies, but carp still present a problem. Fisheries officials may poison the carp again before you read this.

Boats without motors—except electric motors—are allowed on the Upper Lake, Middle Ponds and Lower Lake. The North Marsh is closed to boating.

To contact the refuge office call (702) 725-3417.

CHAPTER 15: Clark County

At an average of four inches of moisture a year, Clark County is Nevada's driest county. In contrast, however, this county is home to more people than almost the entire rest of the state. Most of those people live in Las Vegas. In addition to its 24-hour lifestyle, Las Vegas uses more water per person than Phoenix—as much as 375 gallons per day.

Interstate 15 is the main east-west artery. U.S. Highway 93 connects with Elko, White Pine and Lincoln counties. U.S. Highway 95, on the other hand, runs north along the state's western border.

Las Vegas, obviously, has many of the services anglers need. Henderson, probably the fastest growing city in Nevada, also has many services. Both have a few tackle stores, but southern Nevada's only fly shop is in Las Vegas.

Lake Mead

Nevada's largest reservoir is located near the state's largest population of potential fishermen. Formed by Hoover Dam on the Colorado River, Lake Mead is a short drive from Las Vegas. Take U.S. Highway 93 south from downtown Las Vegas to Henderson, Nevada. Continue on U.S. 93 another 18 miles to reach Hoover Dam. Most of the fishing, however, is accessed by Nevada Highway 147 from Lake Mead Boulevard in Las Vegas, or Nevada Highway 146 from Henderson. North Shore Road connects Nevada 146 and 147 near Las Vegas Bay. Lake Shore Road turns south to meet U.S. 93 near Hoover Dam. Anglers wishing to fish Las Vegas Bay, Callville Bay and the Overton Arm use North Shore Road. Another route involves taking Nevada Highway 169 south from Interstate 15 three miles east of Glendale. This access leads past the Muddy and Virgin rivers to Echo Bay.

Until 1969 Lake Mead was managed as a warm-water fishery; However, the bass were skinny. Threadfin shad, introduced during the 1950s, proved only a temporary solution. Trying to create a sustainable fishery, striped bass were introduced in Mead beginning in 1969. Within ten years, stripers dominated the lake.

Over the last ten years, a predictable balance has developed between striped bass and their primary prey, the threadfin shad. Mead is on the down swing for both striped bass and shad production as of 1996. The up swing should occur again within one or two years. At the end of this cycle the number of shad increase quickly and the number of stripers follow right behind. Most stripers landed today weigh around three pounds. Enough fish in the 10-pound-plus range are taken every year to keep anglers coming back.

During 1993, sub-catchable (less than eight inches) rainbow trout were planted in the Boulder Basin, Virgin Basin and Overton Arm on the Nevada side of Mead. Eight-inch and larger rainbows were stocked at Hemenway Harbor, Government Wash, North Saddle Island Cove, Echo Bay and Overton Beach. The highest harvest and pressure on the trout occurred during December, January and February. Despite the fact that big striped bass eat a few planted trout, anglers want a winter-trout fishery. Jon Sjoberg, fisheries supervisor for Region III, says the trout fishing is primarily a put-and-take situation.

Largemouth bass, black crappie and channel catfish also live in Lake Mead. The largemouth, however, can at times prove as hard to find as the big stripers. The fish are there, but account for less than two percent of creel census data.

With big water like Mead, boats help, but they are not always necessary. Fish Mead from the shore when the shad are in close. Normally that is from August through October. At that time of year anglers can wade or use float tubes to locate the shad and their predators. Boating anglers will find plenty of places to launch. Marinas in most of the areas already mentioned allow the public to launch.

Fly fishing for stripers is more common than some locals believe. J. R. Watkins of Las Vegas did a lot of fly fishing for stripers before he sold his boat. Using a fish finder, Watkins would cruise the lake looking for fish. Once he found them, he would cast a 9- or 10-weight rod rigged with a full sinking line. His minimum tippet strength was 15 pounds. Big stripers try to wrap themselves around bottom brush and break off. Watkins uses Deceiver-style streamers to imitate shad. He uses strong hooks ranging up to size 2/0.

Trolling with minnows and lures produces stripers too. Shad minnows and anchovies are two popular baits.

Most of the big stripers—some in the 50-pound class—are landed during spring and early summer. At this time of year the temperatures are tolerable and fish are spawning.

Mead hosts several largemouth bass tournaments every year. Fully-rigged pros and semi-pros work the lake with all the traditional tackle. A few fly fishermen like Watkins, however, pursue the largemouth with flies. Size 4 and 6 deer-hair and cork-bodied poppers in yellow and black work well. Whitlock's Eel Worm Streamer also catches largemouth.

From boat launches and marinas to resorts, Mead has facilities for every fisherman. Starting at Hoover Dam and going around the Nevada shore look for these facilities; Hemenway Beach has an improved boat ramp; Boulder Beach has a marina with boat launch, a resort and a campground; Callville Bay has a marina with boat launch and a campground; Echo Bay has a marina with boat launch, a resort and a campground; Overton Beach has a marina with boat launch and a campground. For more information contact the Lake Mead National Recreation Area at 601 Nevada Highway, Boulder City, Nevada 89005, (702) 293-8947.

Lake Mohave

Nevada's current big striper water is Lake Mohave. This long reservoir on the Colorado River produced two state records during 1995.

Davis Dam backs up the Colorado River all the way to the base of Hoover Dam and Lake Mead. The result is a long narrow reservoir with a level that fluctuates with the demands of downstream water users.

The upper 20 miles of reservoir is lined by the narrow walls of Black Canyon. Since this portion of Mohave gets cold water from Mead, it is managed as a cold-water fishery. Look for year-round plantings of catchable size rainbow trout in this area.

Willow Beach creel census during 1993 revealed 64 percent of the catch was rainbow trout. Willow Beach is on the Arizona side of Mohave and is reached using U.S. Highway 93 across Hoover Dam. Look for the well marked turn on the road to Kingman. Forty-four percent of the fish kept at Willow Beach were striped bass. The remaining fish were catfish and largemouth bass. Farther south, stripers become the dominant Mohave fish. At Cottonwood Cove, 14 miles east of Searchlight, Nevada on Nevada Highway 164, as much as 90 percent of the 1993 catch was striped bass. Over six percent of the catch was catfish and the remainder was divided between rainbow trout, largemouth bass and bluegills.

Striped bass use the warmer water areas of Lake Mohave for spawning. As the stripers grow, they move into the cold-water areas where they eat planted trout among other things. The main striper forage is threadfin shad, bluegill, green sunfish and crayfish. This cold-water area is known as an excellent place to catch trophy size striped bass.

Use U.S. Highway 95 to access the Nevada side of Lake Mohave. Nelson Landing, Aztec Cove and Placer Cove are reached by taking Nevada 165 through the community of Nelson. While the road to Nelson Landing is paved, a two-wheel-drive vehicle with good ground clearance is recommended for reaching Aztec and Placer Coves.

As already mentioned above, Cottonwood Cove access is via Nevada Highway 164 from Searchlight. South of Searchlight Nevada Highway 163 crosses Davis Dam and enters Arizona. Beyond the dam turn north to Katherine and Katherine's Landing. The other main Arizona access, Willow Beach, has already been described.

Boating anglers have the advantage at Mohave. The upper areas are unreachable from shore and even boaters should proceed with caution as discharges from Hoover Dam can change water levels quickly.

The same tackle and techniques that catch fish at Lake Mead also work at Mohave.

Fishermen have plenty of lakeside facilities at Lake Mohave. Cottonwood Cove on the Nevada side has the only improved marina and boat ramp with lodging and camping. On the Arizona side, Willow Beach has a marina with an improved boat launch and Princess Cove has an improved boat ramp. Katherine, Arizona has a marina with boat launch, lodging and camping facilities. For more information contact the Lake Mead National Recreation Area at 601 Nevada Highway, Boulder City, Nevada 89005, (702) 293-8947.

Colorado River

Below Lake Mohave the Colorado River flows south and west for 12 miles before leaving Nevada. Here water levels change without notice depending on releases from Davis Dam. Normally the river is swift and the water temperatures cool.

Slack water lagoons on the Nevada side are the result of dike construction. This system of dikes lines most of the river length on the Nevada side.

High ground clearance, two-wheel-drive dirt roads also parallel most of the river. Most of these roads intersect Nevada Highway 163 between Laughlin, Nevada and U.S. Highway 93. Laughlin, Nevada and Bullhead City, Arizona are the biggest communities in the area.

The Colorado River fishery is primarily striped bass and rainbow trout. A small warm-water fishery consisting of largemouth bass, bluegill, green sunfish and channel catfish is also available. Rainbows and stripers are the popular fish. Rainbow fingerlings from the Willow Beach National Fish Hatchery are stocked in the river. Some trout fall prey to the stripers, but many remain for anglers.

During spring and early summer, striped bass will run up the river 40 miles from Lake Havasu, Arizona to spawn below Davis Dam. Concentrations of spawners hold in the tailrace below the dam. During the 1970s, striped bass in excess of 20 pounds were caught regularly. Today fish that size are rare.

CHAPTER 16: Getting Around Nevada

It takes forever to get there when going fishing and the end comes too soon once you do get there. Driving home takes a long time, especially if the fishing was less than spectacular.

Scan the streams and reservoirs described here and you will realize Nevada is a big state. Fishing the Silver State means some driving is involved. A lot of driving if you try to explore all of Nevada's fishing. The preceding chapters describe where the fishing is. Deciding which road to take to get there is as simple as looking at a map.

Getting maps of Nevada is easy. The Nevada Commission on Tourism prints a free highway map. Write them at P.O. Box 30032, Reno, NV 89520 or call 1-800-Nevada-8. These maps are also available at tourist and information centers in most of Nevada's larger cities.

Nevada's highway map, good as it is, does not tell the whole story. Stay on the major highways to cover long distances, of course, and when looking for food, gas and lodging. Anglers filled with a desire to explore Nevada's fishing need more than a highway map. For off-road maps, the spiral-bound *Nevada Map Atlas* produced by the Nevada Department of Transportation is excellent. For about $20, sporting goods stores and tackle merchants will sell you one. For more information about this publication write: Nevada Department of Transportation, Map Section, Room 206, 1263 South Stewart St, Carson City, NV 89712. Their phone number is (702) 687-3451.

Detailed topographic maps are also available from sporting goods dealers. Other sources include stores specializing in hiking and backpacking equipment. These maps give fishermen a great amount of detail, which is more than most want. Nevada Atlas & Gazetter was recently released by DeLorme. P.O. Box 298, Freeport, Maine 04032.

The Bureau of Land Management has maps too. Contact the BLM at 850 Harvard Way, Reno, NV 89520 or call (702) 785-6400.

Much of Nevada's better stream fishing is found within forest boundaries. National forest land within Nevada is generally limited to mountain ranges. Between these mountains lies a checkerboard of private and Bureau of Land Management property. Getting information about a particular forest is easy.

Humboldt National Forest

The Humboldt Forest includes the Santa Rosa, Independence, East Humboldt, Schell Creek and the Snake Ranges. Also included are the Jarbidge

Mountains and Ruby Mountains and their wilderness areas. To reach the head-quarters write Humboldt National Forest, 2035 Last Chance Road, Elko, NV 89801 or call (800) 715-9379. Ask for specific information about a region and you will receive everything you need.

Toiyabe National Forest

Within the Toiyabe Forest, anglers will fish the Sierra Nevada from Reno south beyond the Walker River drainage. The Toiyabe and Monitor ranges lay within this forest. Toiyabe National Forest, 1200 Franklin Way, Sparks, NV 89431. Their phone number is (702) 331-644. Like the Humboldt Forest, call or write for specific information.

Desert Driving

Once off the pavement, anglers face a variety of driving conditions. Graded gravel roads allow speeds up to 35 and 45 miles per hour in places. In the broad valleys, roostertails of dust mark other traffic. Changes in conditions, however, come quickly. Sudden turns, dips, cattle guards or stream crossings are guaranteed to get the adrenaline pumping. Cars can and do use the graded roads. Once turning away from these dirt highways, however, cars become a liability. What are described as two-wheel-drive roads in the foregoing chapters require the use of high-clearance pickup trucks. Even these roads can turn into four-wheel-drive roads when wet. The fine dust that can create a contrail in the dry desert sky turn into tire tread filling mud, and can create perilous driving conditions.

Some Nevada anglers carry tire chains for all four wheels of their four-wheel-drive rigs. This is one way to get to the fishing, but it tears up the road for the next fishermen. A better choice is to wait until the road dries out.

Even during dry weather some roads are true four-wheel-drive paths. Steep grades, soft sand and hillside trails await those who like getting there as much as they like the fishing. Vehicle breakdowns, however, can strand even the best off-road driver.

Look closely at the battered old four-by-four of the rancher or miner who lives in Nevada's desert. There is a reason they carry two spare tires. The shovel, chain or sturdy rope and extra gas also serve a purpose. Fishermen exploring the remote corners of Nevada are advised to carry the same equipment. Extra food, water and a first-aid kit round out the well prepared Nevada angler's gear.

Let someone know where you are going and when you expect to return. This simple step can keep a fishing trip from turning into a disaster.

Nevada State Parks

Many of the waters described in this book are on state park land, or are very close to it. State parks offer anglers a clean place to camp and often have hot, running water. For that reason all of the district headquarters are listed here.

NEVADA STATE PARKS

District I, Division Headquarters Capitol Complex Carson City, NV 89710 (702) 687-4370	**District II Headquarters** 1060 Mallory Way Carson City, NV 89701 (702) 687-4379
District III Headquarters 16799 Lahontan Dam Fallon, NV 89406 (702) 867-3001	**District IV Headquarters** Wildhorse State Recreation Area Elko, NV 89801 (702) 758-6493
District V Headquarters P.O. Box 176 Panaca, NV 89042 (702) 728-4467	**District VI Headquarters** 4747 W. Vegas Drive Las Vegas, NV 89158 (702) 486-5126

Desert Camping

A description of the camping is included with each stream, lake or reservoir. However, anglers need to understand what "primitive camping" means. Do not expect picnic tables, water, toilet facilities or cooking facilities. In other words, if you want it, you must bring it. Food, water, shelter and fishing tackle are a good beginning.

One step above primitive, and not much of a step, is a campsite with a picnic table. Some come with a barbecue stand, but many do not. Other facilities are still missing.

Generally, if you pay a fee to camp you will receive more services. Also you will find yourself closer to stores, restaurants and hotels. In Nevada, remote is exactly that.

Nevada Division of Wildlife

A book like this one is impossible to write without the help of professional fisheries biologists. Their work and experience are valuable to all Nevada anglers. While not all regional offices have the ability to provide current fishing reports, they try where money and time allows. NDOW can, however, provide copies of the current fishing regulations. Also, they register power boats and have information on boating safety rules.

NEVADA DIVISION OF WILDLIFE

Nevada Division of Wildlife, State Office
1100 Valley Road
Reno, NV 89520-0022
(702) 688-1500

Region 1 Headquarters
380 W. B Street
Fallon, NV 89406
(702) 423-3171

Region 2 Headquarters
1375 Mountain City Hwy.
Elko, NV 89801
(702) 738-5332

Region 3 Headquarters
4747 Vegas Drive
Las Vegas, NV 89108
(702) 486-5127

Fishing Reports

How is the fishing? What is the best fly? These are the questions on every Nevada angler's mind. The answers are just a phone call away.

What follows is a list of stores that cater to fishermen. This means they usually have an idea about current fishing conditions. Also, they know what tactics are producing today. That doesn't mean conditions won't change by the time you arrive, but at least you have a place to start. To keep their reports current they need your business. Please stop in and give them your report as you head home.

Nevada has only two shops that cater to fly fishermen. The Reno Fly Shop, as you would guess, is located in Reno. Clear Water Anglers in Las Vegas. In between are stores that carry fly fishing tackle and flies. Most are limited, however and few carry fly-tying materials. Still anglers will find some leader material and a fishing report.

FISHING REPORTS

ELKO
Nevada Jim's Outdoor Sports
600 Commercial St., Suite 101
Elko, NV 89801
(702) 753-5467

ELY
Sports World
189 Aultman
Ely, NV 89301
(702) 289-8886

FISHING REPORTS

FALLON
Frontier Liquor & Sporting Goods
1660 West Williams
Fallon, NV 89406
(702) 423-2715

GARDNERVILLE
Angler's Edge
1420 "A" Hwy 395
Gardnerville, NV 89410
(702) 782-4734

HAWTHORNE
Gun & Tackle
P.O. Box 1703
Hawthorne, NV 89415
(702) 945-3266

LAKE MEAD (& Lake Mohave)
Lake Mead National Recreation Area
601 Nevada Highway
Boulder City, Nevada 89005
(702) 293-8947

LAS VEGAS
Blue Lake Bait & Tackle
5485 E. Lake Mead Blvd.
Las Vegas, NV 89115-6709
(702) 452-8299

Clear Water Fly Fishing
3031 E. Charleston Blvd.
Las Vegas, NV 89104
(702) 388-1022

Desert Bait & Tackle
1330 E. Lake Mead Blvd.
Henderson, NV 89015-4636
(702) 564-5660

PYRAMID LAKE
Pyramid Lake Store
29555 Pyramid Lake Road
Suttcliffe, NV 89510-9725
(702) 476-055

RENO/SPARKS
The Gilly
1111 North Rock Blvd.
Sparks, NV 89431
(702) 358-6113

Mark Fore and Strike
490 Kietzke Lane
Reno, NV 89502-1495
(702) 322-9559

Reno Fly Shop
294 E Moana, #14
Reno, NV 89502
(702) 827-0600

Guides and Outfitters

Getting deep into Nevada's wilderness requires dedicated hiking, or a good horse. If you are a hiking angler, you can get all the information you need for the national forest you will be visiting. If, however, you want a horse to pack yourself and your gear into the high country, the following licensed outfitters and guides are available.

GUIDES AND OUTFITTERS

HUMBOLDT NATIONAL FOREST:
JARBRIDGE AND RUBY MTS.
Humboldt Outfitters
HC 60 Box 160
Wells, NV 89835
(702) 752-3714

Elko Guide Service
529 Belloak Court
Elko, NV 89801
(702) 738-7539

Hidden Lake Outfitters
HC 60 Box 515
Ruby Valley, NV 89833
(702) 779-2268

Secret Pass Outfitters
HC 60 Box 685
Ruby Valley, NV 89833
(702) 779-2226 or -2302

Jarbidge Wilderness Guide &
Outfitters
Murphy Hot Springs
Rogerson, ID 83302
(800) 621-0154 or (208) 857-2270

Cottonwood Ranch
O'Neil Route
Wells, NV 89835
(702) 752-3604

TOIYABE NATIONAL FOREST:
TOIYABE AND MONITIR RANGES
Big Smokey Valley Outfitters
HC 60, Box 77206
Round Mountain, NV 89405
(702) 964-1207

Mustang Outfitters
P.O. Box 1149
Round Mountain, NV 89405
(702) 964-2145

Sage-n-Pine Outfitters
1707 Rice Road
Fallon, NV 89406
(702) 423-6171

Businesses, like fishing conditions, change. The names and phone numbers above can change before this book reaches your hands. If unable to locate one of these businesses, use the phone book at your local library. For a current list of licensed guides and outfitters call the appropriate national forest.

CHAPTER 17: A Nevada Angler's Fly Box

In this chapter we examine faith. The faith a fly fisherman has in the fly patterns he or she carries. Yes, this is a chapter about flies, how to tie them and how to fish them, but it also talks about the faith needed to leave them on your leader for more than a few minutes.

Every angler carries a fly box with at least one compartment for experimental flies. Flies that caught fish for someone else yesterday or last week. These patterns get used infrequently, if at all. But the patterns described in this chapter own their place in the fly box. They have paid the mortgage and own their compartment outright. Following are flies that stay tied to my leader.

Nymphs

While many fly fishers prefer to use dry flies, most realize that nymphs, wet flies and streamers catch a lot of fish. Nymph fishing is a challenge, but, with practice, it is extremely effective.

My introduction to nymphing was with the Charlie Brooks or high-sticking method. Simply put, it is casting up-and-across-stream, letting the fly sink as it drifts down to you while lifting line off the water. The dead-drift fishing begins as the fly reaches your position. From this point until the current tugs on the line and leader the fly is in the strike zone. Even when the current pulls on the line and lifts the nymph from the bottom, fish will strike.

Later, I began experimenting with strike indicators. Today the indicator tactic remains in my arsenal, especially when fishing nymphs upstream. For example, on the East Walker River I caught up to 20 trout per hour using a two-fly cast and a strike indicator with a floating line. The indicator was a small Corkie placed roughly four feet above the first fly. A copper bead-head Prince Nymph or weighted Red Fox Squirrel Nymph was the fist fly. I tied a second, two-foot long tippet to the eye of the Prince. On this tippet was a size 14 or 16 Orange and Partridge Soft Hackle. The weighted nymph bounced along the bottom (some of the biggest fish acted like snags) and the wet fly floated just off the bottom. Each fly caught fish in nearly equal numbers.

A two-fly cast works on still water too. While re-visiting many of the reservoirs and lakes described here, I fished a Gold Ribbed Hare's Ear and a Hinkson Monster Midge. The size 14, narrow-bodied and weighted Hare's Ear effectively represents *Callibaetis* nymphs. Tied to the bend or eye of the Hare's Ear hook, the Monster Midge offers an edible alternative. An intermediate full sinking line or a floating line with a 12-foot or longer leader is ideal tackle. A short, nearly creeping retrieve, however, is what appears to make this rig work so well.

Bird's Nest

Cal Bird designed a classic nymph with the Bird's Nest. Cal told me he named the fly while fishing the Truckee River in Sparks, Nevada. This pattern has become a "must" fly for anglers from the California coast to the Rocky Mountains. It is simple to tie and represents all types of fish foods.

When first introduced to the distribution wrap used for the legs, my fly-tying students have some difficulty, but after watching the technique and practicing a little they catch on. Still, some commercial tiers do not use the distribution wrap, but place the hackle legs along the sides of the nymph. Others place a bunch of hackle fibers on top of the hook and another bunch on the bottom. All three methods work.

The original Bird's Nest was brown dubbing and mahogany dyed mallard feather. Since then anglers around Reno persuaded Cal to tie them in black. Olive also produces when conditions warrant.

> **Hook:** 2X long (Mustad 9671), size 10 through 16, weighted
> **Thread:** Color to match body and thorax
> **Tail:** Center section of lemon wood duck flank or dyed mallard flank feather
> **Rib:** Copper wire
> **Body:** Hare's ear and Australian opossum, or other blended fur (favorite colors: black, dark brown, tan and light olive)
> **Hackle:** Remainder of lemon wood duck flank or dyed mallard flank feather
> **Thorax:** Same dubbing used in body.

Gold Ribbed Hare's Ear

The beauties of hare's ear mask as a fly-tying material are many. The spike-like guard hairs trap air bubbles giving the nymph a life-like look in the water. With careful clipping, one mask can yield three natural shades from light tan to dark brown or nearly black. Add a little light Australian opossum and the light shade gets lighter. To make it darker add dark opossum.

Gold Ribbed Hare's Ear nymphs can imitate virtually any insect—mayflies, caddisflies, stoneflies, midges and more. Hook selection and body taper make the illusion work. For example, when fishing nymphs during a *Callibaetis* hatch a weighted, light tan, 1X long size 14 hare's ear works extremely well. Use a weighted 3X long size 10 to represent little yellow stonefly nymphs. Make the stonefly abdomen wider than the mayfly's body.

> **Hook:** 0X, 1X, 2X or 3X long (Mustad 3906, 3906B, 9671, 9672), sizes 8 to 16, weighted
> **Thread:** Light to dark brown, 6/0
> **Tail:** Guard hairs and underfur from hare's nose area or ears
> **Rib:** Fine oval tinsel or copper wire
> **Body:** Blended hare's ear (I blend my own in a coffee grinder. By chopping the hair into 1/4-inch length I can dub tight bodies on small flies.)
> **Wingcase:** Mottled turkey quill (A variation for those with a burning desire to add sparkle is to use dark Flashabou or similar synthetic. Sometimes I leave the wingcase off.)
> **Thorax:** Hare's ear dubbing—noticeably thicker than the body.

Hinkson Monster Midge

Sitting in my boat on Hinkson Slough I watched trout rise sporadically to emerging midges. Some of the midge adults were huge—for midges. We had taken a few fish with Woolly Buggers, leeches and damsel nymphs patterns, but the fish seemed to prefer the midges.

Changing to my pre-strung 2/3 weight rod, I tied a size 12 Monster Midge to the tippet. The leader was 12 feet long and the line was a weight-forward floater. As I let the fly sink I watched the line. Before the fly reached the shallow bottom, the fly line began moving to the right. When the leaps and runs were over, a chunky rainbow came to net with the Hinkson Midge firmly attached to its upper jaw.

That first experience has repeated itself many times on waters all across Nevada. If the fly gets deep enough, then a short, crawling retrieve imitates the swimming action of a midge pupa on the way to the surface. Scud hooks appear to accentuate the squirming, wriggling action of swimming pupae. The nymph hook has less action, but in slow-moving water like the Collection Ditch at Ruby Marshes, the fish seem to prefer it.

> **Hook:** Scud (Tiemco TMC 2457, TMC 2487, or Mustad AC80250BR), sizes 8 to 16
> **Thread:** Black 6/0 or 8/0
> **Tail:** White Poly Yarn, sparse and clipped short (One piece of yarn is used for the tail, wingcase and head. Wrap the body over this piece and cut the tail and head after whip finishing.)
> **Body:** Orvis Body Glass, Vinyl Rib, or Larva Lace (Favorite colors are black, gray, olive and orange/rust)
> **Wingcase:** Same piece of Poly Yarn used for tail twisted tight for a narrow profile
> **Thorax:** Peacock herl
> **Head:** Same Poly Yarn used for tail and wingcase, cut slightly longer than tail and cantered over the hook eye similar to an Elk Hair Caddis. Whip finish between the head and hook eye.

Red Fox Squirrel Nymph

Getting me to try the RFSN took some effort. Sparks angler Mike Muniz bragged about this pattern for two summers before he got me to try it. Now this nymph is a regular on my leader in moving and still waters.

Perhaps it is the color contrast between the rusty, red body and the almost black tail and thorax. I've heard some fly anglers say nymphs and caddisfly worms that have recently molted have similar color contrasts. All I know is this fly works.

For those who follow fly patterns closely, I leave off the hackle legs. I've seen Dave Whitlock tie this pattern, he originated it, but I find the featherless version just as effective.

Hook: 3X long (Mustad 9672), size 6 through 12, weighted
Thread: Dark brown 6/0
Tail: Red fox squirrel gray back guard hair and fur
Body: Red fox squirrel belly fur (can blend in some poly dubbing or Antron for extra sparkle)
Rib: Fine copper or gold wire
Thorax: Red fox squirrel gray back guard hair and fur. Do not chop and blend. Rather, touch dub onto thread and form a dubbing loop. As the dubbing loop is twisted and wrapped around the hook the guard hair stands out to imitate legs.

Pheasant Tail

PTs look like nymphs. The tail fibers lend themselves to a narrow abdomen for nymph tying. As the material is wrapped forward its diameter increases giving a slight, but natural taper. Weight the thorax and build small ramps of thread on both sides of the lead wire to achieve a pronounced taper. Either way this fly looks real. Trout seem to agree.

Hook: 0X or 1X long (Mustad 3906 or 3906B), size 10 through 18
Thread: Brown 6/0
Tail: Ringneck pheasant tail fibers
Body: Same ringneck pheasant tail fibers as used for tail
Rib: Fine copper wire
Wingcase: Ringneck pheasant tail fibers
Thorax: Peacock herl
Legs: Tips from wingcase's pheasant tail fibers pulled back alongside and below the thorax

Prince Nymph

A great searching nymph, the Prince Nymph keeps on catching fish. While many fly fishers carry this pattern in their stream box, they leave it in the truck when fishing still water. This is a mistake. Try the Prince with a floating or full sinking line, you'll like it.

This pattern is easy to tie, so it is within the reach of most tiers. One problem some professional and non-professional tiers have is keeping the ribbing in place after a fish or two. The cause is a steep taper in the peacock herl body, slippery peacock and the oval tinsel. Flat Mylar tinsel stretched slightly as it is wound will last longer. Be sure the hook is secure in the vise jaws before wrapping the Mylar.

> *Hook:* 3X long (Mustad 9672), size 8 and 10, weighted with lead wire, or a gold or copper bead head helps in off-color water conditions
> *Thread:* Black 6/0
> *Tail:* Brown goose biot forked
> *Rib:* Flat gold Mylar tinsel
> *Body:* 3 to 5 peacock herls
> *Hackle:* Brown or gray partridge tied in collar style (1 or 2 wraps). Clip the top and sides if you want.
> *Wings:* White goose biot forked

Wet Flies and Streamers

A safe tactic when approaching new water is to use a Woolly Bugger. This pattern is probably in every fly box that crosses Nevada. The variations are many. Over the years, Pyramid Lake has seen the gaudiest and the biggest. Pyramid fly fishers use a two-fly cast when the wind permits. The tip fly is usually dark with a little flash and occasionally a touch of bright color. The dropper is bright—all white, chartreuse, or pink—with more sparkle and flash.

Small black and olive Woolly Buggers (size 10 and 12) work well in many desert reservoirs like Hay Meadow and Eagle Valley. By adding weight to the front half to third of the hook shank, we can add a jigging action to the fly. A bead at the head will add weight and a bit of color too.

Lake fishing with Woolly Buggers, streamers, wet flies and nymphs often means a full sinking line. The best way to detect a strike is to put the rod tip in the water. When the retrieve stops, all that is required is to raise the rod out of the water to set the hook.

Too few fly anglers use streamers. Olive Matukas, for example, can out-catch Woolly Buggers in many situations. Also, fishing a big Matuka during a midge hatch on still water is a good technique for hooking bigger trout. At

Lahontan and Rye Patch reservoirs, simple marabou streamers imitate baitfish. Predatory walleye and hybrid wipers take them greedily.

Other wet flies, especially soft hackle flies, use materials that move. It is the movement that gets fish to open their mouths. Marabou is a dynamite material when used in damsel nymph and leech patterns.

Funky Bugger

Irv Wheat, professional fly tier and trout keeper at Smith Creek Ranch, developed this pattern. The Funky Bugger is more than just a Woolly Bugger without a hackle. A long shank hook, weighted with 10 to 12 wraps of lead wire and a long marabou tail, represents a leech or minnow. The sparkle body and flash in the tail add to the fly's attraction.

Since the first time I fished the Funky Bugger at Smith Creek, I've tried it on other waters. It has taken fish at Sheep Creek, Wildhorse and South Fork Reservoir. In smaller sizes it worked well at Hinkson Slough and Groves Lake.

> **Hook:** 3X or 4X long (Mustad 9672 or 79580), size 6 through 12, weighted front half to 1/3
> **Thread:** 6/0 color to match tail and body
> **Tail:** Marabou and Crystal Hair (Original by Irv Wheat was olive)
> **Body:** Glo-Brite or Crystal Chenille

Marabou Damsel

This is Randall Kaufmann's pattern. While there are many others, few are as easy to tie or are as effective. Again, marabou equals movement and the Marabou Damsel moves even when you stop retrieving.

Don't wait for a visible damsel migration to try this fly. I've had equally good success by fishing it deep, moderately deep and just below the surface. Many trout will accept the big bite a damsel nymph represents anytime.

> **Hook:** 3X long (Mustad 9672), size 10 and 12
> **Thread:** 6/0, color to match tail and body.
> **Tail:** Various shades of olive marabou—try some golden olive too
> **Rib:** Fine copper wire
> **Body:** Same as tail
> **Wing:** Marabou pinched short

Marabou Leech

Another simple tie that catches fish is the Marabou Leech. Yes, this pattern could represent a damsel nymph or a small minnow. And yes, it is the seductive movement of the marabou that makes this fly so effective.

A hook, marabou and thread are all that is needed. Counting the tail, no more than four bunches of marabou should stick out from the hook. For a slim profile, tie in the tail and cover the extra marabou with thread to about the hook point. Repeat until reaching the eye where one or two wraps of marabou are made around the shank before tying off and forming the head. A fatter fly results from wrapping the shank with marabou forward to the tie-in point of the next marabou wing.

> **Hook:** 2X, 3X or 4X long (Mustad 9671, 9672, or 79580), weight optional, size 6 to 10
> **Thread:** 6/0 and color to match marabou
> **Tail, Body and Wings:** Marabou
> **Flash:** (optional) Flashabou (red with black marabou for example)

Marabou Streamer

Minnows are the preferred forage for big fish. Trout, walleye and wipers all dine on minnows as they grow bigger. While there are many good minnow patterns (streamers), few are as easy to tie as the marabou streamer.

The beauty of this pattern is the way the marabou wing moves. The draw-back, at least in very fast-moving water, is that the supple wing lays flat on the body when under pressure of movement. Fast current means constant pressure. Moderate current to still water means the angler can impart action and make the wing work.

Colors can match traditional streamers. Some of my favorites are the Black Nosed Dace, Mickey Finn and the Black Ghost.

> **Hook:** 3X or 4X long (Mustad 9672 or 79580), sizes 6 and 8
> **Thread:** 6/0, color to match pattern (black for Black Nosed Dace)
> **Body:** Flat tinsel or Diamond Braid in silver or gold
> **Wing:** Marabou (black over white for Black Nosed Dace) the length of the entire hook—eye to outside the bend.

Matuka Streamer

As effective as the Woolly Bugger, the Matuka Streamer is an underutilized fly. One key to this pattern's ability to catch fish is selecting the right feather. Soft, supple, dyed grizzly hen feathers are a must. But more than that, stay away from saddle feathers with pointed tips. Try to find Hoffman Hackle Chickabou. These feathers have wide tips and are ideal for Matuka Streamers and many other wet fly applications.

> **Hook:** 3X or 4X long (Mustad 9672 or 79580), size 4 through 8
> **Thread:** Black or green 6/0
> **Rib:** Copper wire
> **Body:** Black, brown or green chenille
> **Wing:** Two to four dyed grizzly saddle hackles. (Strip barbs from quill where the quill touches the chenille body. Hold wing in place with copper wire rib.)
> **Hackle:** Dyed grizzly hackle

Muddler Minnow

Most, if not all, Nevada streams hold roughfish or minnows. Speckled dace and sculpins are examples. Don't approach one of these streams without a few Muddlers in your fly box. Many times this streamer has pulled a trout out of a dark shadow or deep plunge pool when nymphs and dries could not. If you carry only one streamer, make it a Muddler.

> **Hook:** 4X long (Mustad 79580), size 4 through 10, weighted
> **Thread:** Brown 6/0
> **Tail:** Mottled brown turkey quill section
> **Body:** Yellow fur dubbing or yellow yarn
> **Ribbing:** Overlapping wraps of gold Mylar tinsel
> **Underwing:** Red fox squirrel tail
> **Overwing:** Two matched sections of mottled brown turkey quill
> **Head:** Clipped antelope hair

Soft Hackle

Every time I've started a new fly fisher on moving water it has been with a Soft Hackle. When Michael Leonhardt was 10 years old we went fly fishing on the Truckee River. We turned over stones and I introduced him to the natural food of trout. Then I told him to cast his Soft Hackle into a riffle and let it sink. When you think the fly is under that over-hanging willow, I told him, slowly raise your rod tip. Young Michael did as he was told and a few minutes later we released a 14-inch brown trout.

Soft hackle flies have a dedicated box I carry everywhere. My most productive combinations are; hare's ear with brown or gray partridge; olive hare's ear with brown or gray partridge and black thread; orange floss or thread body, hare's ear thorax and brown or gray partridge; chartreuse floss or thread body, hare's ear thorax and brown or gray partridge.

> **Hook:** Standard length, 1X heavy (Mustad 3906), size 10 through 16
> **Thread:** 6/0, color to match body, or black for most olive patterns
> **Body:** Dubbed hare's ear, rabbit, floss or thread
> **Thorax:** (optional) Dubbed fur as in body
> **Hackle:** One or two wraps of brown or gray partridge.

Woolly Bugger

Is it a leech, streamer, minnow, dragonfly nymph, or what? It is all of these things and more. As described above, this fly is in every fly box in Nevada—except those on the store shelves.

For Pyramid and Walker lakes, the practice is to go big. For smaller desert lakes like Hobart and Hay Meadow most fly fishers use small flies. Color and the amount of flashy sparkle materials are personal preference. Too flashy in very clear water may frighten fish. In murky or muddy water more flash may make the fly work better.

> **Hook:** 3X or 4X long (Mustad 9672 or 79580), size 6 through 12, weighted
> **Thread:** 6/0 to match tail and body
> **Tail:** Marabou (Crystal Hair or Flashabou is optional, but it is effective in Pyramid Lake)
> **Body:** Chenille in black, olive, brown or flash materials like Glo-Brite Chenille or Crystal Chenille

Dry Flies

Even non-fly-fishing anglers have seen fish take insects on the surface. They will say they could have caught more fish if they knew how to fly fish. Perhaps that is why we begin fly fishing.

When we see a fish take our dry fly we know when to set the hook. If fishing a hatch we know what flies to use. But what if there is no hatch? We can beat the water until some suicidal trout takes our offering or we change to nymphs, wet flies, or streamers. On many of Nevada's small streams, fish will take a dry fly almost any time. Two of my favorite small-stream dry flies are the Blonde Humpy and the Royal Wulff.

My fly box holds more dry flies than described here, but these are the most used. If you already have them in your fly box you know why.

CDC Caddis

Unlike the Elk Hair Caddis, the CDC Caddis is meant to lay in the surface film. It doesn't use dry fly hackle for support. The floatation comes from the oil-embedded CDC and the oils of the natural fur. Synthetic dubbing can also aid in floatation.

This is not a rough-water fly. It is, however, a slow or stillwater fly for situations where fish examine the fly closely before deciding to eat it. From small streams to high desert reservoirs, this pattern catches fish.

> *Hook:* 1X fine dry fly (Mustad 94840), size 14 through 20
> *Thread:* 6/0 or 8/0 color to match materials or naturals
> *Body:* Fur or synthetic dubbing to match naturals (favorites are light tan, light olive and olive/gray)
> *Wing:* CDC feather to match natural (leave shoulder as with Elk Hair Caddis)

Hare Dun

Terry Barron, a Nevada angler and professional fly tier, developed this pattern. A variation of the Compara-Dun, the Hare Dun is an excellent *Callibaetis* imitation.

Barron uses a lot of floatant on this fly and dabs off the excess before casting. The floatant allows him to catch and release many fish without changing flies.

> *Hook:* 1X fine dry fly (Mustad 94840), size 14
> *Thread:* Tan 8/0
> *Tail:* Guard hairs and fur from cheek of hare's ear
> *Body and Thorax:* Dubbing of blended light hare's ear and cream Australian opossum, looped
> *Wing:* Tan coastal deer hair

Humpy

They float like cork and look like many winged insects. The Blonde Humpy (yellow thread underbody) can represent a little yellow stone adult, a caddisfly, or a mayfly.

While fishing the Santa Rosa Mountains recently, two different color combinations on a size 14 Humpy caught fish on every stream. Shy brook trout left the shelter of undercut banks to intercept our flies. Brown trout took them without hesitation. The blonde version has been in my fly box for better than 20 years and it still catches trout.

> *Hook:* 1X fine dry fly (Mustad 94840), size 10 through 18
> *Thread:* 6/0 color for underbody
> *Tail:* Elk hair, light to dark
> *Body:* Elk hair over layer of tying thread
> *Wing:* Tips for elk hair body divided and posted
> *Hackle:* Ginger; grizzly; grizzly and brown, or color to match hair

Joe's Hopper

From late September through mid-November grasshopper patterns can produce exciting dry fly fishing. Joe's Hopper is my favorite because it is easy to tie and catches fish. Some tiers may not approve of the water absorbing chenille body, but this pattern catches trout even when sunk.

Use stout tippets, 3X and 4X, when casting to fall spawning brown trout. Smack the water when delivering the fly and hold on. The take will be sudden and hard.

> *Hook:* 2X long (Mustad 9671), size 10
> *Thread:* Black 6/0
> *Tail:* Red hair (calf tail, dyed deer, etc.)
> *Butt:* Yellow chenille or yellow poly yarn looped over hair tail
> *Rib:* Brown saddle hackle sized to hook and clipped on sides
> *Body:* Chenille or yarn used for butt
> *Wings:* Matching sections of mottled turkey quill
> *Hackle:* Brown and grizzly dry fly hackle mixed

Parachute Adams

This chapter is not ignoring the traditional Adams dry fly. Rather, the goal is to get you to carry a few Parachute Adams' for lakes and slow-water conditions.

By dubbing the body and thorax all the way to the thread head, we present fish with a complete silhouette. True, using the wing post to tie in the hackles and to whip finish is a tricky maneuver. The result, however, is a fly that is more durable and effective.

> *Hook:* 1X fine dry fly (Mustad 94840), size 12 through 18
> *Thread:* Black 6/0
> *Tail:* Mixed grizzly and brown spade hackle fibers
> *Body and Thorax:* Gray muskrat dubbing
> *Wing:* White calf tail or white poly yarn posted
> *Hackle:* Grizzly and brown tied parachute style (tie-in on wing post, wrap
> from top of posting thread down to body, tie off at body and
> whip finish—all on the wing post)

Quiggley Cripple

This is the "after-the-hatch" fly. Once the *Callibaetis* have hatched and the adults flown away to mate, a few cripples remain. Trout continue to cruise, looking for stragglers and cripples. Give them something to dine on. Try the Quiggley Cripple in gray or light tan like the Hare Dun.

> *Hook:* 1X fine dry fly (Mustad 94840), size 14 through 18
> *Thread:* Black 6/0
> *Tail:* Gray marabou tips
> *Body:* Gray marabou used for tail
> *Rib:* Tying thread
> *Thorax:* Gray muskrat dubbing
> *Wingcase and Wing:* Gray deer hair (wingcase is clipped at rear, tight to
> muskrat thorax and wing is cocked at about 45 degrees over hook eye)
> *Hackle:* Grizzly (three wraps at point where deer hair is tied in)

Royal Wulff

Brook trout are suckers for bright flies, or so New England writers tell us. In the alpine reaches of Nevada's high mountain streams, the Royal Wulff is king. Even rainbow trout willingly take this pattern.

The small streams of the Ruby Mountains are a good example. On the heavily fished lower reaches of Lamoille Creek, Royal Wulffs consistently catch fish.

> *Hook:* 1X fine dry fly (Mustad 94840), size 14 through 18
> *Thread:* Black 6/0
> *Tail:* Dark brown elk hair
> *Butt:* Peacock herl
> *Body:* Red floss
> *Shoulder:* Peacock herl
> *Wings:* White calf tail divided and posted
> *Hackle:* Coachman brown

NEVADA

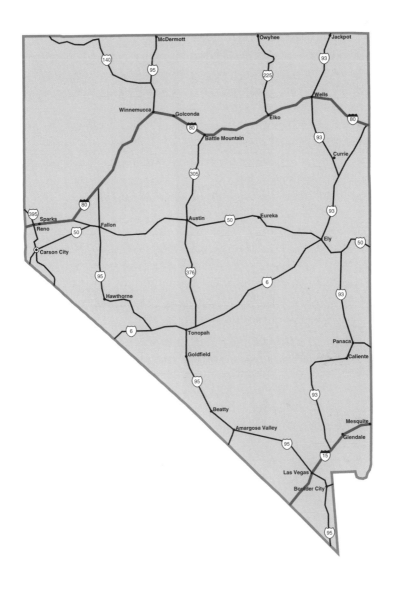

Bibliography

—*Nevada Map Atlas*. Carson City, Nevada. Nevada Department of Transportation, 10th Edition, Rev. 1993

Castleman, Deke. *Nevada Handbook*. Chico, California. Moon Publications Inc. Fourth Edition, 1995

Dennis, Jack. *Jack Dennis' Western Trout Fly Tying Manual*. Jackson Hole, Wyoming. Snake River Books. 1974

Hafele, Rick and Dave Hughes. *Western Hatches*. Portland, Oregon. Frank Amato Publications, Inc. 1981

La Rivers, Ira. *Fishes and Fisheries of Nevada*. Reno, Nevada. University of Nevada Press. 2nd Edition, 1994

Lanner, Ronald M. *Trees of the Great Basin: A Natural History*. Reno, Nevada. University of Nevada Press. 1984

Moreno, Richard. *The Nevada Trivia Book*. Baldwin Park, California. Gem GuidesBook Co. 1995

Mozingo, Hugh N. *Shrubs of the Great Basin: A Natural History*. Reno, Nevada. University of Nevada Press. 1987

Roush, John H. Jr. *Enjoying Fishing Lake Tahoe, The Truckee River and Pyramid Lake*. Chicago, Illinois. Adams Press. 1987

Stetzer, Randle S. *Flies, The Best One Thousand*. Portland, Oregon. Frank Amato Publications, Inc. 1992

Sigler, William F. and John W. Sigler *Fishes of the Great Basin: A Natural History*. Reno, Nevada. University of Nevada Press. 1987

Trotter, Patrick C. *Cutthroat Native Trout of the West*. Boulder, Colorado. Colorado Associated University Press. 1987

Much of the background for this book comes from Nevada Division of Wildlife fisheries reports. Fisheries management plans and progress reports by fisheries biologists across the state proved invaluable in producing this work.